SHORT CUTS

INTRODUCTIONS TO FILM STUDIES

OTHER TITLES IN THE SHORT CUTS SERIES

THE HORROR GENRE

FROM BEELZEBUB TO BLAIR WITCH

PAUL WELLS

WALLFLOWER

LONDON

CONTENTS

LIST OF ILLUSTRATIONS

ACKNOWLEDGEMENTS

I would like to thank the following people for their contributions both to this book, and the Sony award-winning radio series *Spinechillers:*

The Horror Crowd: Clive Barker, Doug Bradley, Jo Brand, James Cameron, Ramsay Campbell, Angela Carter, Wes Craven, David Cronenberg, Sean Cunningham, Brian De Palma, Jonanthan Demme, Robert Englund, Ruth Fainlight, James Ferman, Jodie Foster, Richard E. Grant, James Herbert, Steve Jones, Christopher Lee, Stephen King, Nigel Kneale, John McNaughton, Ingrid Pitt, Kate Pullinger, Sam Raimi, George Romero, Ken Russell, Paul Schrader, Ridley Scott, Stephen Spielberg, Richard Stanley, Quentin Tarantino, Robert Wise.

The Critics: Christopher Frayling, Barrie Gunter, Peter Hutchings, Mark Jankovich, Alun Jones, Mark Kermode, Kim Newman, Andrew Tudor, Linda Ruth Williams.

The BBC Folk: Anne Hinds, John Powell, Jane Ray (Above and Beyond!), Dave Slingsby, Polly Turner, the BBC Radiophonic Workshop, Focus Groups in Basingstoke, Bradford, Hull, London and Wrexham.

The Supporters: The staff and students of the Media and Cultural Studies departments at De Montfort University in Leicester and the University of Teesside. Further, my thanks go to all the staff at Wallflower Press.

This book is dedicated to my wife Joanne, my own 'little monster', Freddie, and my best friend, Simon, all of whom have seen me through a few horrors of my own!

INTRODUCTION

Terror is the feeling which arrests the mind in the presence of whatsoever is grave and constant in human sufferings and unites it with the cause.

– James Joyce

Like many people interested in the horror film, or indeed comedy, its allied genre, I view its analysis as something which should not strain too far after meaning for fear it might undermine the sensation created. Having said that, in one form or another, I have done exactly that, and still been frightened half-to-death or giggled helplessly in the cinema on numerous occasions. Thankfully the effects of horror or humour initially by-pass the inhibitions and intrusions of the intellect so the thrill can precede the theory.

This short study, based principally on the research undertaken for the BBC Radio series *Spinechillers: A History of the Horror Film*, and enhanced by further work on undergraduate courses, seeks to introduce readers to the horror genre in a variety of ways. In the first section, *Configuring the Monster*, I will explore the key themes of the genre, the main issues and debates raised, and engage with approaches and theories that have been applied to horror texts. This theoretical background will be presented via the *modernist** context within which early horror texts evolved. This brief description of the generic development of the horror film will thus provide

---

* terms indicated with an asterisk throughout the book are defined in the Glossary

a review of its fundamental preoccupations, especially through a discussion of a variety of psychoanalytic and gendered readings. This first part also includes a case study that reviews indicative patterns of readings of horror texts across different age groups that are interesting in terms of the progression of spectator involvement with horror film.

In the second section, *Consensus and Constraint 1919–1960*, and the final section, *Chaos and Collapse 1960–2000*, I will further address the chronological evolution of the horror film, looking at how it has reflected and commented upon particular historical periods. This analysis will consider the role of both traditional myth and gothic literature in early cinematic representations of horror. Post-war developments are then reviewed in terms of the revisiting of these generic formulae. The more contemporary transgression of boundaries of permissible *gore** and pathological states are then considered through a discussion of the work of postmodern auteurs reworking the genre's field of operation and its consistent recycling.

Inevitably in a work of this length, many complex arguments will be rendered briefly and simplistically, and many important observations reduced to description and generalisation. This is not a disclaimer, rather it is an encouragement for other researchers to pursue further lines of enquiry and to address the genre anew from a personal, informed perspective.

1   CONFIGURING THE MONSTER

A modernist context

The history of the horror film is essentially a history of anxiety in the twentieth century. In the way that fairytales, folktales and gothic romances articulated the fears of the 'old' world, the contemporary horror film has defined and illustrated the phobias of a 'new' world characterised by a rationale of industrial, technological and economic determinism. Arguably, more than any other genre, it has interrogated the deep-seated effects of change and responded to the newly determined grand narratives of social, scientific and philosophical thought.

Fred Botting has suggested that at the end of the eighteenth century, 'gothic narratives ceded to the ambivalence that shaped them and became increasingly uncertain of the location of evil and vice ... the locus of evil vacillates between outcast individuals and the social conventions that produced or constricted them' (1996: 90). As the nineteenth century passed into the twentieth, this prevailing moral and ethical tension between the individual and the socio-political order was profoundly affected by some of the most significant shifts in social and cultural life. This effectively re-configured the notion of evil in the horror text – soon to be a cinematic as well as literary form – in a way that moved beyond issues of fantasy and ideology and into the realms of material existence and an overt challenge to established cultural value systems.

The late nineteenth century also saw the development of several significant and transformative social discourses. Among these were the theories of political economy as advanced by Karl Marx in *The Communist Manifesto* (1848). These were concerned with proletarian identity and power in the face of the commercial objectives of an emergent industrial and capitalist society. Marx's views posited the necessity of a class struggle, in the light of the potential estrangement of the working class into an increasingly alienated condition. This perspective becomes especially important in relation to the horror film because the natural benefactors of the social infrastructure were a bourgeoisie who maintained the traditional codes of cultural elevation, enacting lives of privilege and enpowerment, while exploiting those creating the material conditions by which this was possible, and who benefited little from it. Arguably the horror film implicitly embraces the leftist critique of this process, consistently invoking the 'monster' of the alienated and disadvantaged as the key protagonist against bourgeois middle-class orthodoxies. From *Nosferatu* (1922), to *Frankenstein* (1931), to the period gothics by the Hammer and Corman studios, to *Night of the Living Dead* (1968), to the films of Jesus Franco and Alejandro Jodorowsky, the genre has been used to explore modes of social 'revolution' in which naturalised ideas about bourgeois orthodoxy are transgressed, exposing how the 'working class' in Weimar Germany, Depression-era America, Franco's Spain and so on have been oppressed and socially manipulated to maintain those advantaged by the late capitalist status quo.

These issues may be intrinsically related to the ways in which the ideas expressed in Charles Darwin's *On the Origin of Species* (1859) entered the public domain. Darwin saw evolution as a process of natural selection, and proposed a hierarchical notion of human development and status – essentially 'the survival of the fittest' – which challenged established Christian orthodoxies and fuelled imperialist assumptions of racial superiority. Darwin argued that natural selection 'is a power incessantly ready for action, and is immeasurably superior to man's feeble efforts as the works of Nature are to those of Art' (1859: 53). He continues to play out issues about the way in which humankind seemingly 'artificially' imposes itself upon the conditions of material existence, while nature slowly but surely, organically, and often invisibly, changes the world: 'Man selects only for his own good; Nature only for that of the being which she tends ... He often begins his selection by some half-monstrous form; or at least by some modification prominent enough to catch his eye, or be plainly useful to him. Under nature, the slightest difference of structure or constitution may well turn a nicely balanced scale in the struggle for life, and so be preserved' (71–2). This tension becomes a key theme in the horror film in a variety of ways. From the monstrous metamorphoses in films like *Dr Jeckyll and Mr Hyde* (1931) to the anthropological imagination of *King Kong* (1933) and to the *Creature Features** of the 1950s Cold War and the cycle of *revenge of nature* films, including Alfred Hitchcock's *The Birds* (1963), the genre has explored the ways in which humankind has engaged with the processes of the natural order.

Darwin's ideas, although significantly challenged, and in some aspects disproved, nevertheless underpin this theme, providing a context in which the apparent restlessness and indefatigability of nature is pitted against the will to power of humankind. The phrase 'will to power' has particular purchase in relation to the work of philosopher Friedrich Nietzsche, who argued that humanity was subject to spiritual crisis and a constant process of degeneracy, foregrounding its own inherent desire to impose order and facilitate destruction within an entirely secular contemporary context. 'I have drawn back the curtain on the depravity of man,' wrote Nietzsche, continuing, 'I call an animal depraved when it loses its instincts, when it chooses, when it *prefers* what is harmful to it' (1985: 117). Nietzsche insists that humankind is entirely nihilistic, and that 'nothing in our unhealthy modernity is more unhealthy than Christian piety' (119), suggesting 'in Christianity neither morality nor religion comes into contact with reality at any point' (125). This collapse of spiritual and religious values in the face of the seemingly indifferent progress of 'modernity' also chimes readily with the horror film.

Nietzsche's relativist stance implies that there is no certainty to existence; that humankind lives in an amoral universe, merely subject to a series of conflicts and confrontations, a process of one imposition upon another, without any true consensus. Arguably, this may be *the* fundamental theme of the horror film – in which the 'monster' (whether it be *Dracula* (1931), the spawn of the devil in *Rosemary's Baby* (1968), the possessed child in *The Exorcist* (1973), or the supernatural presence in *The Blair Witch Project* (1999)) represents the archetypal struggle, not merely between 'good' and 'evil', but for the presence of an 'order' which seeks to evidence and maintain the idea that there is someone or something to believe in which justifies material existence. The overwhelming currency of the horror film errs to the view, however, that the Nietzschian perspective is true – 'modernity' has in effect sacrificed the possibility of faith and purpose to arbitrariness and apocalypse. This socio-cultural context is thus bound to give rise to a deep psychological, emotional, and physical malaise; one embraced, defined, and explained in the work of Sigmund Freud.

It is the work of Freud (see 1986c), and the emergence of psycho-analysis, which fundamentally changed the ways in which humankind perceived itself. His investigation of the structures of consciousness revealed levels of a more 'primal' existence beneath the observable codes of socialised behaviour. He suggested that repressed and un-addressed feelings were at the heart of unconscious thoughts, and that dreams often revealed meanings about the true nature of human identity. Ironically, psychoanalysis itself has been used as a tool by which to understand cinema, predicated upon the view that films operate in a similar way to dreams, revealing issues which cannot be explicitly cited or have been displaced into another form. Inevitably, the horror film has been subject to a great deal of psychoanalytic criticism, which will be explored later in this discussion, but at this stage it is sufficient to say that Freud's ideas have served to underpin a self-consciousness in the genre which has deliberately engaged with 'madness', 'dysfunctionality', and 'psychosis' as key aspects of the horror text. The 'monster', as it were, is 'all in the mind'.

These various factors constitute the framework for the defining principles and themes of the horror genre in the modern era. Simply, all these grand narratives – social alienation, the collapse of spiritual and moral order, a deep crisis of evolutionary identity, the overt articulation of humankind's inner-most imperatives, and the need to express the implications of human existence in an appropriate aesthetic – may be viewed as the conditions which underpin contemporary horror texts.

The writers and film-makers who followed in the influential wake of twentieth-century modernity have therefore explored the fears which arise in the contemporary world, and what it is to be frightened. They are the authors of the new fables and fairytales which persist in revealing primal wisdom and collapsing traditional hierarchies. Consequently, the contemporary horror film continues in its own generic tradition of playing along 'boundaries between fictional forms and social rules' (Botting 1996: 170), oscillating between a sometimes highly politicised critique of the modern world and a playful engagement with its own conventions to facilitate its own postmodern freedoms.

Horror films as texts

Horror films have been analysed within a range of theoretical paradigms and discourses. The genre has been addressed in the light of its theological and moral perspectives, its sociological and cultural dimensions, its politics of representation, and its configuration as a set of texts particularly conducive to psychoanalytic approaches. Problematically, the horror genre has no clearly defined boundaries, and overlaps with aspects of science fiction and fantasy genres. Also, in recent years, many of its generic elements have been absorbed into the mainstream thriller. Arguably, there is no great benefit in attempting to disentangle these generic perspectives. It may be more constructive to proceed on the basis of addressing the distinctive elements of any one text within a particular historical moment.

It may be noted that the horror genre is predominantly concerned with death and the impacts and effects of the past, while science fiction is future-oriented, engaging with how human social existence could develop and dealing with humankind's predilection for self-destruction. While science fiction is potentially utopian (although often critically grounded), the horror genre is almost entirely dystopic, and often nihilistic in outlook.

Science fiction is more concerned with the external and macrocosmic, while horror is arguably preoccupied with the internal and microcosmic (see Sobchack 1987 and Locanio 1987).

The fantasy genre, however, is based on re-imagining the world in a more playful or utopian guise, while only temporarily moving out of (endorsing) the terms and conditions of the status quo. Again, while the horror genre possesses aspects of this approach, it rarely leaves the status quo unaffected, and in many cases represents a subversive or alternative perspective on issues of gender, race, class, ethics and social context. It should be further stressed that there is no great uniformity in either the narratives or pre-occupations of the genre across the years, and that it accomodates a superfluity of topics, which in themselves demand different responses and call upon different critical perspectives.

Devils and doubles

Central to the horror genre's identity is the configuration of the 'monster', which has been redefined with each development in social and cultural history. The monstrous element in the horror text is usually an interrogation of the amorphous nature of evil, or an address of the limits of the human condition; physically, emotionally and psychologically. The prevailing archetype of the monster is the Devil, the symbolic embodiment of evil that is a constituent element in monist religions and which appears in various forms in myths from across the globe (see Babuta and Bragard 1985). In many senses, the theological struggle between good and evil played out in the horror text – most overt, for example, in films like *The Exorcist* (1973) – becomes a conceptual umbrella for struggles between law and order, the sacred and the profane, barbarism and civility, truth and lies. These dialectical positions are addressed through one of the dominant motifs of the horror text: the *doppelgänger*. This is effectively a 'double', in which humankind confronts its nemesis either through the opposition of an individual and a monster or by the exposure of the two competing sides of an individual – normally, one rational and civilised, the other uncontrolled and irrational, often more primal and atavisitic.

This duality may also represent a conflict between competing sexualities, gender orientations, repressed desires and their expression, or may be a more obvious and confrontational antithesis between the powerful and powerless.

Psychoanalyst Otto Rank wrote of 'Der Doppelgänger' in 1914, suggesting that the double was essentially the way in which the soul or ego sought to preserve itself, ensuring against destruction by replicating itself. Bound up with a narcissistic self-love which is self-protecting and strongly predicated to the denial of death, this act of 'doubling' can work in reverse. Once the double is cleaved or threatened, it heightens the degree by which mortality and the signs of death are enhanced. It is of no surprise, therefore, to see the prominence of the motif in the horror text.

Metaphors and mayhem

The horror genre has become increasingly concerned with the relative and fragile nature of existence. Although the monster may be understood to operate within the doubling framework on many occasions, it is pertinent to conceive of it as a metaphor; a projection of particular threats, fears and contradictions that refuse coexistence with the prevailing paradigms and consensual orthodoxies of everyday life. The monster may also be perceived as a direct and unfettered expression of the horrors that surround us. It comes to represent the disintegration or de-stabilisation of any one dominant perception or understanding of what it is to be human. Stephen Neale (1980) argues that the double is ultimately the delineation between the human and the non-human. Further, in a psychoanalytically-determined view of the monster, he suggests that the monstrous is a projected fear of castration and its disavowal.

In whatever way the monster is conceived and acts, however, it serves to operate as a mode of disruption and breakdown in the status quo. A major theme of the horror genre is therefore the expression of the ways in which individuals try to maintain control of their lives in the face of profound disruptions which only comment on the frailties and brutalities of the status quo and its habitual norms. Fundamentally, then, horror texts engage with the collapse of social/socialised formations. These range from the personal to the familial, the communal, the national, and the global. Any one level of identity can be impacted upon by the monster, and either radically changed or annihilated. These formations are the very structures which offer humanity a sense of purpose and order; their collapse is an indication that they either exclude, cannot contain, or misrepresent forces which ultimately re-visit and challenge them. This occurs in many ways, and the metaphor of the monster can adequately depict these forces, whether they are in effect 'the beast within' (see Grixti 1989) or 'the other' from without (see Wood and Lippe 1979). Arguably, if established social and historical frameworks preserve purpose and order in human endeavour, they also come to define the terms and conditions of life itself, and the implied promise of the finite and eternal. The collapse of these frameworks is thus at the heart of the horror text.

Fundamental fears

The horror genre is predominantly concerned with the fear of death, the multiple ways in which it can occur, and the untimely nature of its occurrence. The central generic image of the corpse reminds the viewer of extinction. Anxiety arises, thereafter, from the conceptualisation of the 'un-dead', which resists the notion of finality and demonstrates the perpetual agonies of a non-corporeal or sub-human existence. In this model, every monster is the promise of death and demise, and crucially, 'difference'. Consequently, the 'un-dead', or 'the dead that walk' (Halliwell 1988) are intrinsically symbolic forms, literally embodying states of 'otherness' which are intrinsically related to humanity but are ultimately a parallel and threatening expression of it.

This theme effectively makes the horror genre continually relevant because societies are constantly having to address the things which threaten the maintenance of life and its defining practices. These may be obvious and clear – terminal disease, acts of violence, accident and so on – but there are often other factors which seem to make life a wholly contingent issue, and elements which can bring chaos to what was previously a known and highly controlled environment. For example, Stephen King lists ten key fears that underpin most horror writing: fear of the dark, 'squishy' things, deformity, snakes, rats, closed-in spaces, insects, death itself, other people, and fear *for* someone else (cited in Underwood and Miller (1986: 10)). Horror texts are grounded in the reproduction and creation of the emotion of fear which arises from these conditions. The fear of *when* something life-threatening may occur, and *what* may produce it – essentially the deep-rooted fear of the unknown – is closely linked to other primal anxieties. This becomes crucial in any definition of horror and the related conditions created within and experienced through such texts.

Nineteenth-century gothic novelist Ann Radcliffe suggests, 'terror and horror are so far opposite, that the first expands the soul, and awakens the faculties to a high degree of life; the other contracts, freezes, and nearly annihilates them' (1826: 149). In this model, terror stimulates the desire to actively come to terms with shock; to enjoy its provocation and understand its effect. There is a sense of transcendence in 'terror' which may be related to notions of the sublime, where the primordial or natural order may be recognised, acknowledged and awed. Furthermore, Edmund Burke, in *A Philosophical Enquiry into the Origin of our Ideas of the Sublime and the Beautiful* (1757), suggests that natural events or environments which exhibited vastness and grand design provoked awe and wonder in the human sensibility, but simultaneously reminded humankind of its diminished and limited status, thus engendering terror within a potential state of tranquillity. In many senses this apparently contradictory response characterises the ambiguity of feelings which may be at the heart of engaging with the idea of 'difference' which is central to many horror texts. Horror, however, has only a negative and paralysing effect; a wholly nihilistic and enduring condition of death and oppression. Radcliffe's definition is enabling in the sense that texts may be viewed in the light of 'terror' and its potential radicalism, or 'horror' and its creation of a seemingly reactionary position.

Nigel Kneale, writer of the television series *The Quatermass Experiment,* later filmed as *The Quatermass Xperiment* (1955) suggests:

Horror is what you might feel if you went, for example, into a jungle, or a place where you had lost all your bearings, where you were no longer sure of anything. A place where you began to suspect that there was something present which you couldn't pin down; something which you wouldn't be able to identify but which would be dangerous and could destroy you.[1]

Here, it seems, is the paralysing effect implied by Radcliffe. The horror text clearly calls upon these *inherent* human anxieties. Such fear of the unknown is intrinsically related to the fear of the dark, simply because any potential threat remains unseen. Paul Schrader, writer and director of *Cat People* (1982), a remake of Val Lewton and Jacques Tourner's 1942 classic, wished to explore this idea:

I wanted to evoke dream creatures that are tied to our genetic information. Those black cats that jump from the trees and white horses galloping that still come back to us in our dreams. I have to believe that this is very ancient information because one of the reasons why the panther was so feared was because you couldn't see him, and by the time you could, he had struck.

This perspective alone neatly encapsulates the relationship between primal anxiety, its metaphoric recall in dreams, and the capacity for the horror text to accommodate and illustrate this process. Writer of supernatural fiction H. P. Lovecraft further formulates this scenario in more detail:

Man's first instincts and emotions formed his response to the environment in which he found himself. Definite feelings of pleasure and pain grew up around the phenomena whose causes and effects he understood, whilst around those which he did not understand – and the universe teemed with them in the early days – were naturally woven such personifications, marvellous interpretations, and sensations of awe and fear as would be hit upon by a race having few and simple ideas and limited experience. The unknown, being likewise the unpredictable, became for our primitive forefathers a terrible and omnipotent source of boons and calamities visited upon mankind for cryptic and wholly extraterrestrial reasons, and thus clearly belonging to spheres of existence whereof we know nothing and wherein we have no part.

This primordial world, when perceived as a physical environment, has facilitated the horror film with numerous creatures, particularly reptiles, vermin and insects. These 'monsters' share the planet and operate as part of a natural world that humankind is increasingly divorced from or has taken for granted. This parallel set of life-forms constitute a potent challenge if they behave in any way which is not in the thrall of human control. Their sense of otherness is informed by their unfamiliarity, the visual and tactile repulsion they can engender and the power they possess in surviving in the light of the exigencies of the great chain of being. Humanity's position at the top is precarious indeed. The primordial world essentially acts as a parallel order to the modern environment, providing an often incongruous interface. The monsters of the primordial world are not merely other creatures, but ill-fitting ancestral psychological, emotional and physical imperatives which may not find a ready context in the modern era. The horror text is thus often grounded in this context, prompting a deeper recognition of the required consensus and constraint needed to achieve even the most basic model of civilisation.

Empathy and identification

Ultimately, and particularly in the post-1960 period of horror films, the greatest fear which has been addressed is the fear of *other people*. As Jonathan Demme, director of *Silence of the Lambs* (1991) has claimed, 'at the moment the one thing that is able to utterly and uncomplicatedly fill us with true terror is the *serial killer**, because we know that any of us could be a victim for whatever serial killer is seeking our type of person'.

Indeed, the serial killer has become the staple villain of the post-*Psycho* (1960) horror film, either in the guise of the machete-wielding automaton or the seemingly unmotivated boy-next-door. Ostensibly, the serial killer individuates a dehumanising process and operates within the horror text largely as an 'abstraction' which distracts attention from the damaging social phenomena and historical antecedents which produce him. Further, in some senses the serial killer, however abstract, gives name and identity to the increasingly incomprehensible violence and brutality diffused through contemporary life (see Seltzer 1998).

Interestingly, the predominant models of the serial killer in real life are murderers of children, sexual partners and prostitutes, and it is clear that in many instances these actions constitute an assault on familial and social structures that marginalise the individual. Jodie Foster, in researching her role as Clarice Starling in *Silence of the Lambs*, comments, 'serial killing is a way of thinking in which violence is an answer to everything'. The serial killer's background is often characterised by childhood sexual abuse, and his actions are motivated by the need for power, status and recognition. Such notoriety, and indeed, celebrity, is afforded by the serial killer's symbiotic relationship with the media, a relationship which offers a fascination to a public ready to engage with the 'reality' of brutal excesses and the seemingly inexplicable forces which underpin them. Arguably, it is the very 'abstraction' of the serial killer which makes him a relevant symbolic icon for the systematic destructiveness of contemporary culture. For example, John Amiel's *Copycat* (1996) self-reflexively shows a serial killer aping the killings of 'famous' serial killers, aptly illustrating their currency in the modern consciousness of the late twentieth century (see Wilson and Seaman 1990; Taubin 1991; Dyer 1997).

Allied to this is perhaps the greatest of fears, and one that the horror film concentrates on creating. This is the fear *for* other people. James Cameron, director of *Aliens* (1985), sought to combine a range of these fears in his film, suggesting 'there are a couple of scenes which deal directly with the fear of a tight space with some sort of lethal presence – here an insect-like predator – which remains unseen but you know it's there. This is related to another fear that I played on intentionally which is the parent's fear for their child – here Ripley with Newt'.

Issues concerning empathy and identification are fundamentally bound up with the construction of the horror text, and will be further explored later, both in the ways that theorists have configured the audience as a subject, and through some material gleaned from a reception study.

It will be argued that the 'fright' experienced by any one viewer is intrinsically related to the level of commitment he or she has to simultaneously fearing for the protagonist under threat and intuitively relating to the fear represented in the presence and danger of the antagonist (the monster). This feeling is inherently contradictory and ambiguous because it is a responsive emotion which demonstrates a desire to protect someone from harm, allied to the vicarious pleasure of perceiving the impactive (and painful) outcome of threat upon them. The tensions between pleasure and pain are both the subject of the horror text and the object of its fascination for audiences. In this vein, Joel Black notes that 'our reactions to these fictional representations... may range from horror to admiration, but whatever shock we experience will consist of aesthetic astonishment rather than of moral outrage' (1991: 9). It may be pertinent to slightly modify Black's point and suggest that this 'aesthetic' response may merely precede moral outrage and not replace it. These tensions are central to the key psychoanalytic approaches to the horror film and are dealt with in the next section.

Freud for the afraid

The touchstone for many perspectives in this area is Sigmund Freud's essay on 'The Uncanny' (1985c).[2] Chiming readily with the points already raised by Kneale and Schrader, and with the writing of Lovecraft, Freud suggests 'the uncanny is that class of frightening which leads back to what is known of old and long familiar'. Analysing the terms *heimlich* ('homely') and *unheimlich* ('unhomely') in the light of E.T.A. Hoffman's version of the ancient tale of 'The Sandman', Freud suggests that the uncanny arises from the ways in which the unfamiliar impacts upon the understanding and acceptance of the familiar. In Freud's terms 'the unfamiliar' is actually the 'secretly familiar', something which has gone through the process of repression, but on some occasions returns, and consequently threatens a human ego which has constructed itself as secure from the uncertainties of the external world. Tracing this to a number of sources, including primordial states, infantile complexes, and experiential transformations, Freud in essence articulates a duality which echoes the concept of the *doppelgänger* cited earlier. Indeed, at a simplistic level, most psychoanalytic approaches which take up the motif of the uncanny are seeking to define the terms and conditions of the oppositional dualities which are played out in the metaphor of the monster and its context in horror films.

In a highly influential post-Freudian approach Julia Kristeva (1982) takes up the concept of 'the abject' as her presiding model. Kristeva's work addresses Freud's conception of the human subject and suggests that instead of having a fully-formed, highly 'familiarised' mature ego, which is perceived as an ideal state, the human subject has a fragmentary, unstable ego which is always partially formed. This unstable ego is fundamentally undermined by the recognition of the consistent collapse of the perceived ideal because of a detrimental repulsion to the functional aspects of the body. Bodily emission, waste and malfunction – the most self-evidently 'taboo' aspects of the body – become evidence of humankind's perpetual decay, and operate as persistent signifiers of eventual death. This highly negative position articulates images of abjection in the horror film as a particular model of 'the return of the repressed' in which the monster is a relentless reminder of a collapse of the illusory and seemingly valueless 'self'. It is a formation which offers little hope, in the sense that it is clear that the self can never rise above this on human terms, and moreover, gains nothing from the process of repression and possible release. The duality Kristeva explores is only about the inevitable determinism of the self as a symbolic process of functions and their outcomes, and carries with it no sense that the social context can be influential or affecting. Crucial to her approach is the idea of a fear of the 'archaic mother', which significantly genders Freud's primordial approach, and constitutes a key influence on Barbara Creed's address of the concept of the 'monstrous feminine' as it appears in horror texts (see Creed 1993).

In essence, then, the 'abject' and 'abjection' are terms used by Kristeva to describe the effects of destruction, decay, disease and defilement, which expose the limits of human control in relation to the onset of death. Kristeva usefully deploys the concept of the 'border' to delineate the ambiguous area between life/death, repression/release, and control/ disruption. Again, this may be seen within the framework of doubles and dualities discussed earlier, which represent the tension between the human subject and the monster. Further examples of this may be seen elsewhere. James Twitchell (1985) argues that the monster is effectively a representation of deep adolescent anxiety as the child moves towards sexual maturation, thus articulating a tension between the loss of childhood 'wholeness' and the fundamentally flawed condition of the adult. Robin Wood (1986) advances an important distinction between basic repression (the repression necessary to live as a civilised human being) and surplus repression (the ideological repression imposed by the culture) as a key undercurrent, especially in the contemporary American horror film. He suggests that surplus repression creates a society of 'monogamous heterosexual bourgeois patriarchal capitalists' and any-thing which operates outside this or is simply different from it is a configuration of otherness. Consequently, Wood's determination of the monster is a quintessentially political version of the 'return of the repressed', and thus differs slightly from Kristeva's configuration. Thomas Elsaessar (1989) suggests, however, that the notion of the 'repressed' should be seen not merely as a political or psychoanalytic issue, but one which enables monsters to be configured in a way that reveals the transformation of history into the form of the uncanny and fantastic.

Creed's work takes up Kristeva's concept of the 'archaic mother' in Ridley Scott's *Alien* (1979), and addresses a number of films in which women are played out as the monster: a victim of satanic possession in *The Exorcist* (1973), the embodiment of 'a monstrous womb' in David Cronenberg's *The Brood* (1979), a vampire in Tony Scott's *The Hunger*

(1983), a witch in Brian De Palma's *Carrie* (1976), and 'castratrice' in Alfred Hitchcock's *Psycho* and Meir Zarchi's *I Spit on your Grave* (1978). Creed's work is especially persuasive in locating women in more complex paradigms than merely that of the 'victim', and moreover exposes the deep anxiety in predominantly male directors concerning the personal and social impact of women upon men, the construct of the family, and the patriarchal system. David Cronenberg, for example, describes *The Brood* as 'my version of *Kramer vs Kramer*. It is a clear projection of my feelings about divorce; violent possessive emotions, and the decaying nature of what were once highly positive feelings of love and desire' (see Handling 1983; Drew 1984); Rodley 1992; Traube 1992).

In the period after *Psycho* (1960), but anticipated as early as *The Bad Seed* (1956), the family has been perceived as increasingly dysfunctional; the locus for incest, abuse and other Oedipal angst. Indeed, the domestic space has become *the* locality for the worst of horror. In a gradual process from the monster movie with its obvious gothic trappings, through to what Barry Keith Grant (1996) calls 'yuppie horror', the horror text continually addresses the dysfunctional and antithetical aspects of the romantic and the domestic, collapsing all received notions of predictable gender identities and social formations.

Carol Clover's (1992) feminist perspective maintains the idea of dominant gender paradigms, however, through her conception of 'the final girl' who takes on the (masculine) monster in the contemporary 'slasher' movie. While some (female) viewers see this as an act of empowerment, Clover argues that these final women are only acting in the same ways that male protagonists would, and this 'phallic' charge both undermines their feminine address, and their (often literal) role as 'castrator'. The slasher movie – effectively a narrative in which a machete-wielding monster causes seemingly indiscriminate havoc by brutally murdering a group of young people – has often been seen as a metaphor for the punishment of young people involved in illicit and casual sexual practices. The sexual dimension of these films is further heightened by psychoanalytic readings which project the monster as masculine, playing out castration anxiety. Women, so the theory goes, must be eliminated in the horror text because they *lack* a phallus, and threaten men by projecting and potentially affecting the same lack upon them. This position remains highly questionable at a number of levels. The monster sometimes has an indeterminate gender, or is, indeed, a woman. Further, when men and women 'fight back' it is largely in fear of life itself, and not wholly predicated on issues of sexual anxiety from either gender. Clover's definition of 'the final girl', therefore, in characters like Nancy in *Nightmare on Elm Street* (1985), Jennifer in *I Spit on your Grave* and Alice in *Friday the 13th* (1980) as a 'phallic' heroine, is questionable. These are not quasi-men, literally castrating male figures. They often distinguish themselves by not merely rejecting the established tenets of masculine behaviour, but enhance their credentials as modern *post-feminist* women by moving beyond both the traditional/generic expectations of women, and feminist/psychoanalytic orientations.

It is perhaps useful here to step back from this approach. It reveals a tension between the persuasiveness of psychoanalytic positions and more literal interpretations. Arguably, the methods, violent or otherwise, by which the monstrous adversary may be defeated are not clearly gendered, and mostly operate as circumstantial reactions to threat. The often basic implements employed, or instinctive blows struck in the 'fight' with the monster are more to do with the ostensibly primitive limits of conflict within the horror text than their gendered implications. The act of resistance is thus more important than the tools and tensions of its execution in securing the support of, and empathy with, a viewing audience.

A useful intervention may be drawn from the work of Elisabeth Bronfen, who shifts the psychoanalytic emphasis from the 'phallus' and the pre-eminence of the castration narrative, to privilege the centrality of the 'navel'. Significantly, 'this knotted scar ... commemorates the loss of the mother but also marks our mortality, the vulnerability of our bodies, and thus radically protests against any phantasies of omnipotence and immortality' (1998: xii). Simply, and especially in the post-1960 period of the horror film, both monster and victim may be best understood by 'the knot' of their own highly distinctive and often unknown motivations and desires, rather than the social codings imposed upon them. Arguably, this is why in the post-*Psycho* era, the monster and its effects remain perpetually shocking. It is only potentially rationalised on its own terms, rather than those which have been so obviously socially determined. In using psychoanalysis to emphasise issues of mortality, and not issues of 'lack' which have been played out on the feminine subject, Bronfen changes the nature of how gender, sexuality, and sexual behaviour may be understood within the horror text.

Increasingly, the dominant readings of the relationship between the monster and a potential victim have been further problematised by an address of the issues of sex and sexuality underpinning their exchanges. Rhona Berenstein and Harry M. Benshoff have given full account of the ways in which classic horror texts have facilitated 'queer' readings, an engagement with '*camp*'*, and the playing out of same-sex relations and alternative sexualities. Berenstein suggests that 'the traditional names given to sexual orientations among humans – heterosexual, homosexual and bisexual – do not convey fully the contours of the fiend's attachment's to its victims' (1996: 24), and adds, crucially, 'that in the figure of the monster, presumptions of sexual difference on the basis of biology are as fraught with ambiguities and are as historically constructed as are those based on gender attributes (29). Importantly, the condition of 'asexuality' also figures prominently within the genre, especially in relation to the creation of ostensibly 'human' forms outside the exigency of the human reproductive system. Consequently, the biological determinacy of sexual codes and practices may be absent, and require other forms of interpretation.

While the horror film has always enacted fantastical and subversive scenarios which operate with high social relevance – cannibalism, for example, used as a metaphor in 1970s horror to expose the ways in which a capitalist economic order 'feeds off' the less powerful and socially mobile, or 1980s AIDS anxieties in teen-vampire pictures like *Near Dark* (1987) and *The Lost Boys* (1987) (see Taubin 1995) – it has also become engaged with the real and material conditions of existence. While filmmaker and novelist Clive Barker argues that 'horror is still the last refuge of the surreal', theorist Jonathan Lake Crane suggests, 'in irrevocably linking horror to the unconscious we dismiss, all too hastily, the possibility that horror films have something to say about popular epistemology, about the status of contemporary community, or about the fearsome power of modern technology' (1994: 29). Lake Crane argues for a more socially-orientated set of readings which take into account the idea that the horror film is more closely related to the terrors of everyday life, and actually speaks to audiences in a highly direct fashion.

Horror films in context

This more literal perspective leads readily into the address of how these monstrous fears and their construction may be understood outside the predominantly psychoanalytic framework. For example, Mark Jankovich has suggested that 'psychoanalysis has a built-in tendency to produce interpretations which not only have little but no relation to one's actual experiences of a text, but actively contradict those experiences' (1992: 12). However, it is clear that the psychoanalytic approach still impinges on a more literal understanding of the audience and its social context in a number of ways. The *frisson* of the horror text for the audience is underpinned by the expressed desire to experience feelings which relate to taboo agendas and the limits of gratification. This is a 'given' of the genre's appeal – horror fans enjoy the pleasure of being frightened and enjoying emotional extremes. It can be further argued that much of the 'psychobabble' associated with the horror film has entered the public domain, and is often clearly understood by fans, simplifying the notions of what is on offer for the audience and why it supposedly enjoys horror films.

Many areas which may be understood as previously only the domain of the unconscious are now conscious, known, and readily addressed, so the factors which actually affect audiences may be of a different order than those suggested in the 'dualities' explored earlier. Much has been written, for example, about the nature of catharsis which an audience can experience. Catharsis is a concept first formulated by Aristotle in his *Poetics* where it is suggested that in watching dramatic tragedy a spectator experiences pity and terror, and therefore has a beneficial 'purgation' of emotions which is necessary and purifying. This theatrical model of purgative feeling is related to annual community rituals which sought to rid the culture of the impact of sin and death in the previous year. This was often conducted through a period of celebration in which *carnivalesque** modes of subverting and reversing the established codes and conventions of social existence were played out (see Aristotle 1920; Bakhtin 1984).

Although the use of the term 'catharsis' is problematic in some respects, it may be simply understood in what Stephen King describes as the 'playing out of basic drives, wishes, and primal feelings *by proxy*'. These feelings may be of a sexual, violent or fetishistic nature, and again may be assumed to have been repressed or diminished by the socialising and civilising processes of the society in which the viewer has been brought up.

The construction of the 'fetish' or 'fetishised' objects in the horror text often works in a spirit where the monster operates as a collage of elements which constitute a wholeness that seemingly resists notions of vulnerability and anxiety. Roger Dadoun (1989) argues that the fetish is a signifier of totality, phallic security, sexual determinism and ritual in the face of competing elements which would undermine these factors. Clearly, figures like Dracula, Michael Myers, and Freddie Krueger may be configured in this respect: the illusory autonomy of the monster and its context often re-determines or ignores the contingencies of the social world. It is therefore not surprising that the horror film has flourished in periods of social difficulty or collapse because it offers the wholeness of the monster, the enigma of its meaning, and a dissociated context to engage with. While any audience experiencing catharsis or 'fetishising' the monster is questionable at the collective level, it may be, as Stephen King argues (perhaps with some degree of self-promoting hyperbole), that 'for every five or ten members of your audience which is getting rid of something through what a horror movie is doing, there are bound to be one or two, of a highly conducive sensibility and background, who are taking in something they need, the fuel for violence, sadism, you name it'.

Such issues have inevitably informed debates about the limits of the horror text, and consequently, matters of classification and *censorship** which emerge from them. For the most part, this debate has centred on the nature of graphically depicting (often sexually-related) acts of violence and what some would argue are offensive or distasteful images. Moreover, concerns have been raised about the nature and effect of these images upon audiences, with the implied anxiety that showing such material may encourage some members of the audience to behave violently and anti-socially. Classification and censorship have thus become crucial issues for film-makers, critics and audiences alike, provoking exchanges which have ranged from arguments for the necessity of complete freedom of expression, through to the call for the complete banning of the most extreme texts. These have become more than issues of taste and acceptability, and have moved into complex areas concerning the role of art in a democratic society, and the on-going perception of the horror genre as a worthless product of popular culture, appealing only to lowest common denominator responses.

The media-contrived moral panic which focused on 'video nasties' in the 1980s, and the concomitant effects of the Video Recordings Bill (1984), as well as the furore that surrounded the supposed influence of *Child's Play 3* (1991) on the brutal murder of James Bulger by two young boys are merely two instances of this relationship and its implications. The Bulger case, for example, focused upon three key areas that are most cited in the discussion of these issues: that those who have a predisposition to act violently are encouraged by these texts, that there is a tendency to mimic or play out 'copycat' violence as it is depicted in such texts, and that these kind of texts encourage a desensitised view of the violence enacted upon victims.

Self-evidently, any one of these perspectives is open to question. Arguably, they concentrate too much on the centrality of the 'effect' of any one text, at the expense of a proper consideration of the extensive social influences of any one individual. Further, they imply that 'aesthetic' effects are indistinguishable from related events and their possible repercussions in reality, and may be understood simply as clear cases of cause and effect. This is, of course, simplistic, but nevertheless an oft-cited paradigm about horror films, which serves to 'scapegoat' them in a way that ignores the cultural context from which they emerge, and defines them as an easy explanation for insoluable social ills. A consistent concern is that horror films are harmful to children, but clearly these films are not made for children, and the responsibility for who views them lies with adult authority figures who determine how and when horror films are seen. If horror films are watched within the domestic space, for example, it is surely the parent who actually 'classifies', 'categorises', and 'censors' material – the lockable cupboard is a far more practical censure than the ideologically charged social machination that insists upon changes in horror fictions, or indeed, their banning.

Arguably, if the horror text is to be culturally and historically pertinent, film-makers have to engage with an aesthetic space free from the moral and ethical obligations of the social paradigm in which they live – only then can they comment upon, and critique the conditions of, the material world. If the social concern about violence in horror films is to be properly addressed, for example, it is crucial that such issues be treated responsibly, looking at violence as a reality, and not the titillatory experience of the adventure spectacles which pass uncensored into cinemas every week. The horror text does this in a variety of ways, and this is why, as a genre, it remains subversive and challenging because it foregrounds, through the comparative safety of fiction, the very agendas humankind needs to address in 'fact'. While this remains contentious, and subject to considerable opposition, the horror film makes us confront our worst fears, our more perverse feelings and desires, our legitimately complex 'darker' agendas, and in this it serves an important function as a progressive and sometimes radical genre, in the face of increasingly reactionary stances.

The debates in these areas are ultimately too complex and sensitive to summarise fully here, but it is clear that perhaps more than any other genre the horror genre is predicated on the relationship between viewers and texts. The *actual* points of stimulus, possible influence, imitation, and behavioural inflection which are alleged to occur because of the specific narrative and representational aspects of horror films are the very subject of this discussion. These are the aspects which raise the status of the horror film from its lowly, often marginalised, and sometimes pilloried position to one which may be viewed as art, and as a relevant social phenomenon which requires a level of debate and interpretation which is not merely about the potential intricacies of psychoanalytic formulations, but about 'real world' knowledge and practices (see, for a fuller discussion of this important area, Phelps 1975; Barker (ed.) 1984; Barker 1984; Dewe Mathews 1994; Medved 1994; French 1996; Kermode and Petley 1998).

As the horror genre has developed it has inevitably changed, but remains highly correspondent to the social and cultural upheavals to which it runs parallel. Just as inevitably, it has often been the subject of debate and controversy because of the very subject area it is dealing with. At a superficial level, if the purpose of a horror film is to frighten its audience, such an objective seems to have little redeeming social merit. The nature of how and why horror texts become 'entertaining' is therefore a crucial area of discussion. The most important point to note before any such analysis can be undertaken, however, is that no conception of 'the audience' as an entity is relevant here, and even the notion of analysing socially and historically specific audiences as a more apposite way of understanding reception is problematic. As Stephen King implies in his views on catharsis, it may be the case that matters of taste, preference and experience may only be understood through individual sensibilities, competencies and levels of access to texts, with the implied coda that any generalisations must be greeted with scepticism.

This seemingly creates an impasse which is difficult to negotiate. Consequently, I wish to provide one model offered by Noel Carroll, which places the audience in a position of spectatorship which may be read as universally appropriate to most audience paradigms (see Carroll 1990) and offer my own highly limited model which uses a number of focus groups to discuss their experiences of the genre. Echoing Boris Karloff's distinction between the real life horror of a car accident and the fantasy of highly artificial cinematic 'frights', Carroll seeks to locate an audience within what he describes as 'the emotion of art-horror' – the fundamental feelings and dominantly signified positions that the horror text is *supposed* to illicit through the ways that characters are constructed to provide cues, instructions and models of behaviour for audiences to respond to. 'Works of horror', he suggests, 'teach us, in large measure, the appropriate way of responding to them' (1990: 31). Carroll also makes a sharp distinction between the monster as an impure and contradictory concept, and a natural phenomenon, thus excluding people and creatures, whose monstrousness can be given clear definition under religious, scientific, medical or political codings. Further, Carlos Clarens suggests that this is essentially the difference between the 'visionary' and the 'psychological' (1967: 13). This differentiates, for example, Franken-stein's monster from Norman Bates in *Psycho*, or the zombies in *Night of the Living Dead* (1968) from Hannibal Lector in *Silence of the Lambs*. While this does not prevent Bates, Lector *et al* being interpreted in a metaphorical, or interstitial light, it assures a necessary ambivalence of discourse in the way that the monster is perceived. In being outside scientific cultural categories, the range of responses to the monster are signified by the characters experiencing its effects, but remain sufficiently open to prompt individual responses in the audience.

Carroll argues that the response to the monster as it is constructed through the characters is a 'cognitive-evaluative' emotion; an emotion that at once *provokes* feeling but *invokes* a reason for it. For example, Veronica, Seth's girlfriend in Cronenberg's *The Fly* (1986), embodies all of the audience's feelings towards Seth as he mutates into 'Brundlefly'. From tactile repulsion right through to empathetic sympathy and affection, the audience is offered its vocabulary of responses. How each member of the audience uses or responds to the vocabulary is inevitably varied, but such a vocabulary, which creates 'the emotion of art-horror', is present in all horror texts, and may be usefully deployed in articulating subject positions in the rest of this discussion.

In contemporary genre study, the role of the audience has become increasingly important. In a study of this length it is not possible to do justice to this area of inquiry, but in order to test some of the prevailing assumptions about the horror film, a small study was carried out with a number of focus groups of various ages, backgrounds, and levels of participation to evaluate how people actually engaged with, understood, and potentially acted upon their relationship with horror films. While this has a number of methodological shortfalls, it nevertheless articulates the dominant thoughts and pertinent issues which extend the nature of the argument, and encourages further study of how a horror film can provoke complex feelings, social criticism, laughter, and dread.

Old ham or new flesh?

This audience sample was based upon four focus groups, each composed of twelve people, six of each sex, categorised in the following age bands: 16–25 years, 25–40 years, 40–55 years and 55–80 years. Selection for each group also took ethnicity and social background into account to facilitate a wide range of opinion concerning a range of topics. These included stating the most frightening moment from a horror film, the behavioural impact and enduring effects of having seen particular horror texts, the reasons for having a horror genre and wanting to watch horror films, the perceived limits of the genre, and the changing nature of the genre over time.

Elements of feedback were broadcast as part of the six essays constructed for *Spinechillers* (BBC Radio), a cultural history of the horror film. Some of the most significant outcomes can be summarised as follows:

16–25 years: Earliest film cited: *The Exorcist* (1973). Most recent film cited: *Jurassic Park* (1993).

The viewers within this group displayed a ready engagement with, and appreciation of, the *spectacle* of horror films in relation to the scale of violent action and the amount of blood-letting and gore depicted. There was clear acknowledgement, however, of the artifice of the action, and a scale of appreciation which admired innovation and imagination in this area suggesting that the more extreme, exaggerated and gratuitous the events were, the *less* alarming the lack of genuine motivation driving them was, because the pleasures arose from the excess more than the narrative.

Allied to the clear acknowledgement of the artifice of the medium was a strong desire to know how special effects were created and a heightened admiration of industry figures like Tom Savini and Dick Smith. A related issue here was a stated commitment to the works of particular directors (for example Romero, Cronenberg, Raimi, Argento) or to specific cycles (*A Nightmare on Elm Street*, *Friday the 13th*, *Halloween* and so on). This led on to the purchase of popular genre-related publications like *Fangoria*, *Shivers* and *Shock Xpress*, and participation in web sites dedicated to particular directors, films, exchanges of opinion, and new horror fictions written by fans themselves.[3]

Stress was placed on the importance of humour in relation to scare effects, and was clearly a strong determining factor in the perception of the genre as 'entertaining'. However, monsters were often dismissed as unpersuasive if they stretched too far in the area of comic address. Comedy was also perceived as a clear mitigating factor in the acceptance of extreme scare effects and the potential levels of brutality. Horror texts were more often seen in the light of black humour or the 'grotesque'. Furthermore, a clear distinction was made between effective and ineffective scare effects. This was largely concerned with the immediacy of physical effects (i.e. things which made you jump) and what were described as more *persistent* effects where imagery recurred in dreams, or reminded viewers of 'real world' frights or phobic conditions. Lastly, the group recognised itself as a 'video generation' who enjoyed watching horror films both on their own and in social groups, as well as in the cinema. They felt that they had a special identity as fans of the genre, who intrinsically understood the textual and extra-textual meanings of the films and their making.

Michael O'Pray has argued that 'material which meshes horror and humour is more likely to be identified with the grotesque' (1989: 256). Further, Mary Russo suggests 'the grotesque body is open, protruding, irregular, secreting, multiple, and changing; it is identified with non-official low culture or the carnivalesque, and with social transformation' (1994: 8), and consequently constitutes a model of 'grotesque realism' which in its openness, flux, and overt display of processes and functions collapses socio-cultural distinctions. The excessive re-orientation and display of the grotesque body operates in a way which is amusing, because of its incongruous relationship to the socially-determined limits of body and identity, but horrific because it violates the classical norms and orthodoxies of bodily representation, rendering both the unknown interiority and external 'completeness' of the body as wholly arbitrary (see Paul 1994). The group above informally embraced these issues, and clearly revelled in the liberation they felt in the interpretation of the imagery.

25–40 years: Earliest film cited: *Night of the Living Dead* (1968). Most recent film cited: *Silence of the Lambs* (1991).

There was a clear recognition of a slow disengagement from the genre as the group aged. The viewers within this group displayed a strong wish for the horror film to regain a seriousness of purpose and relevance and uniformly felt that many films of the mid-1980s were facile and predictable. Moreover, the group felt that the humour was crass and ill-suited to the genre, predicated only on attracting a younger audience and enhancing marketing practices. Women, however, felt a strong sense of increasing empowerment as more horror heroines resisted the traditional role of victim, exposed the limitations of men and their attitudes, and attempted to (often ingeniously) defeat the monster.

A general point was raised concerning the un-persuasiveness of British horror compared to its American and European counterparts. 'Pinhead' from *Hellraiser* (1987) was cited as an effective monster, but actually not as frightening as Frank, the figure in bodily flux.

40–55 years: Earliest film cited: *House of Wax* (1953). Most recent film cited: *Halloween* (1978).

FIGURE 1 *Psycho (1960)*

The viewers within this group displayed vivid recollections of the colour of blood in the Hammer films, and a uniformly favourable set of general comparisons between the versions of the Frankenstein and Dracula narratives from Hammer and their Universal Studios' counterparts.

Christopher Lee and Peter Cushing were strongly admired as the epitome of 'Englishness'. Furthermore, strong memories of the effectiveness of *The Quatermass Xperiment* were reported, because of its established presence on television and the desire to see the monster in Westminster Abbey, where the Queen's coronation had taken place, 'on the big screen'.

Also mentioned were memories of 'gimmicks' at cinemas, such as 'Emergo', the flying skeleton, to accompany William Castle's *The House on the Haunted Hill* (1958), 3D glasses for Andre De Toth's *House of Wax* (1953) (one person recalled that the director himself could not see the 3D effect because he was blind in one eye), fangs being handed out before Dracula films, and signing insurance forms that guarded against 'death by fright'.

Psycho was continually cited as a film that was genuinely shocking, disturbing, and clearly different from previous horror films. There were recollections of audience members fainting and being sick during the showing, as well as announcements and publicity materials asking audiences not to reveal the ending. The group categorically stated that it was the first horror movie which they could not forget, and felt frightened when they thought about it even within the apparent safety of their own homes.

Essentially confining 'contemporary' horror to *The Exorcist* and *Halloween*, the group felt that these films were too violent and often unacceptable in their content. A number of women felt that *The Exorcist*, for example, was not really about good and evil, but the persecution of a child, and that this was neither valid nor entertaining.

55–80 years: Earliest film cited: *Nosferatu* (1922). Most recent film cited: *Dead of Night* (1945).

The viewers within this group consistently referred to the inter-activity between the audience and the protagonists on the screen, particularly in relation to warning potential victims of the presence of the monster. The group demonstrated a particular preoccupation with the way that the horror film configured the night as an especially dangerous time, and how frightening it was to walk home through poorly-lit streets after a horror film. Vermin were particularly cited as frightening because they were often seen as part of the poor social conditions in which the viewers lived: films seemed to turn small, familiar but unpleasant things into large-scale monsters.

A clear concern was registered about the ways monsters violated notions of law and order and how this in itself was upsetting. In general it was felt that people were 'good' and law-abiding, and a nostalgia was noted for an earlier period of life in which traditional courting rituals included men taking women to a horror film in order to 'protect' them from the threat of the monster during film showings. Lastly, experiences in World War Two clearly compromised the desire to watch anything that was horrific or frightening in the post-war period.

Although these points are clearly selective and emerge from the dominant aspects of conversation, they offer some pertinent observations about the changing nature of the genre and its context. Ironically, the more graphic and, arguably, more realistic the images in horror films from the 1970s through to the 1990s have become, the more an increasingly 'knowing' audience recognise their artifice and contrived purpose. The monster movies of the 1920s and 1930s, dismissed by latter-day audiences, clearly had a personal and social effect on their viewers, and seemingly operated as a reminder of the real world and its conditions. Older viewers, perhaps inevitably more conservative in their tastes and outlooks, set clear limits to the value of a horror film, and enjoyed experiencing the menace of the monster before its ultimate containment. Furthermore, the horror films of the 1950s and 1960s operate as a watershed in this respect, and constitute a period of transition in which the tensions between cinematic artifice and 'real world' issues are heightened, becoming more contra-dictory and ambiguous concerning the nature of their pleasures.

All the groups demonstrated a high degree of inter-activity with the films they watched; either verbally, physically, discursively, or extra-textually in their later behaviour. Moreover, all groups perceived a relationship between horror and humour, and noted that laughing about what is frightening is a good way of dealing with it, although all the groups stated that the seriousness of certain films and the *intensity* of feeling caused was sometimes lasting. However, one of the most significant problems here remains in *how* viewers read and interpret texts, as there is clearly a crucial movement both within the texts and outside them between the metaphorical and the literal. Literal readings inevitably concentrate on the surface, graphic depictions of events, but do not necessarily move on to their metaphorical, metaphysical, and indeed, *actual* implications. That is to say, literal interpretations sometimes neither acknowledge the symbolic weight of the material nor suggest that the scale of violence or explicitness shown has genuine correspondence to the excesses of real events. Generationally, there seems to be a tendency for older people to engage with texts within their social context, and for younger people to see texts only as important in themselves. Further, older audiences seemed less willing to engage with an aesthetic which is not located in a mainstream context, dismissing films outside conservative parameters as either in poor taste or poorly executed.

An interesting parallel here is that considered interpretation is often accorded by critics to big-budget quasi-horror films like, for example, *Aliens* or *Silence of the Lambs*, but almost uniformly does not inform low-budget or self-evidently exploitative material. It is this which audiences are most often highly responsive to and, crucially, that which often constitutes the next mainstream cycle. Scholars and cultural champions of the horror genre have done much to redeem this view in recent years, and texts which may have been completely ignored, dismissed, or confined to oblivion have been reclaimed (see Newman 1988; Benshoff 1997; Jankovich 1996). This is not to suggest that every horror text is of equal worth, but that many of those which have been subject to easy rejection have more to say to audiences than has been acknowledged.

One of the difficulties that presents itself in the horror genre, and which is arguably both justification for and mitigation against its significance, is its consistent preoccupation with articulating and expressing the worst of personal and social ills. Confronting the monster is either perceived as untenable, unpersuasive or risible in the horror film, or conversely, as an approach which merely recalls the horrors of the real world and should be avoided at all costs. 'Who needs more misery?', the argument goes. 'Isn't there enough on the news?' This both damns and praises the genre, suggesting at one level, that it is so unrelated to life as we know it that it is effectively pointless, while at another level, acknowledging its relevance and effect. The latter position most readily chimes with an endorsement of the metaphoric capability of the horror genre and its capacity to accommodate complex themes in a comparatively straightforward yet all-encompassing way.

The horror text, it seems, is consistently testing the implications of the behaviour of humankind, the impact of late industrial capitalism, the effects of historical determinism and the enduring influence of the need to preserve some notion of moral order, social value, and consensual justice. A horror film is therefore always about the shifting parameters of good and evil. 'Shape-changing' is a chief determining concept at the heart of the horror film, whether this be in the metamorphoses of the monster or the context in which it exists. Nothing is certain; all the benchmarks of normality and the preservation of the status quo are being interrogated and re-defined, both within and without the text.

One of the greatest appeals of the horror text for audiences, therefore, is the way it examines the tension between materiality and imagination; a tension that readily echoes the freedoms of childhood play and the testing of social limits. This is not to suggest that a horror text is wholly about the regression to childhood pleasures and openness, but it is clear that some of the playfulness in horror texts is concerned with the ways that imaginative constructs test the recognisable limits of concrete, objective, and normative codes of the material world. This is both satisfying and potentially traumatic and can be related to the ways in which 'suspense' is constructed in the horror film, and to the tension between horror and humour. This will be examined in more detail below, but it is clearly the case that terror and comedy have many similar traits, and often differ only in their outcomes. There is a fine line between the scream of fright and the scream of laughter, and film-makers have often used this proximity for further challenging effects. Indeed, once the horror film moves into the postmodern era its chills translate into chuckles with increasing frequency, as film-makers bring irony and pastiche to the conventions of the genre for an increasingly 'knowing' audience.

This is partly an acknowledgement of the transience of the mechanisms and material used in any one appropriation of the horror text. Edison's version of *Frankenstein* (1910) will not work in the same way as Universal's 1930s versions, Hammer's 1950s vehicles or Kenneth Branagh's 1994 film (see Kermode and Kirkham 1994), either for the audiences who originally saw them or for the audiences who experience them after their moment of production. To shock an audience is increasingly difficult, and this has provoked more ingenious ways of manipulating and creating effects, and necessitated a more considered and more realistic exploration of even darker themes. Those horror texts which continually invoke the obvious strategies to create predictable sensations in an audience have become films about film-making, and are predicated on the understanding that horror fans are versed in the appeal of mechanistic formulas and the artifice of special effects. Ironically, this is when the horror genre, despite its supposed extremes, becomes highly conservative and reassuring. Though it remains exploitative, the level of address becomes little more than a playing out of adolescent issues and pre-occupations. The horror text that remains 'adult' still carries with it the complex psychological, emotional, physical and ideological charges of ancient folklore, fairytale and myth. In illustrating and commenting upon the deep-seated anxieties of its time, the horror film thus performs a necessary social function, for to challenge and disturb is to insist upon a liberal democratic process that both reflects and critiques its socio-cultural moment. Although seemingly nihilistic in outlook, the horror film can continually remind an audience of the things about which it should neither be complacent nor accepting.

2 CONSENSUS AND CONSTRAINT 1919-1960

Vapors, odd beings, terrors and deluded images

It is customary to trace the origins of the horror film in nineteenth-century gothic literature, but before we engage with some of the more influential factors of this tradition, the history of the horror text can be located more specifically within the realm of fairy tale and myth.

Writing in 1949, leading authority on myth Joseph Campbell suggested that 'the symbols of mythology are not manufactured ... they are the spontaneous productions of the psyche' (1988: 4). The concept of the monster can be located within this context, which represents the spontaneity and evolution of the 'vapors, odd beings, terrors, and deluded images' that constitute the monstrous within the 'feared adventure of the discovery of the self' (8). Further, in addressing the way that myth is grounded in the tension between tragedy and comedy, Campbell suggests that 'tragedy is the shattering of the forms and of our attachment to the forms; comedy, the wild and careless, inexhaustible joy of life invincible' (28), and that myth should lead from the former to the latter.

Although the horror film does not entirely fulfil the same function, it is clear that the monster operates in a manner which shatters form and familiarity, and ultimately offers the possibility of comic redemption. This is why, following the brutal stabbing of a nurse by a marauding Michael Myers in *Halloween II* (1981), in which she hangs precariously, spiked on a large knife, the audience laughs as her clogs clatter to the floor seconds later. Furthermore, comic redemption comes in finding previous horror texts, and their terrors, somewhat camp and increasingly risible.

These readings are perhaps based on what Berenstein has suggested is the fundamental 'centrality of performance' (1996: 8), particularly, within the horror text, in regard to gender. The more an audience engages with the artifice of the *performance* of gender traits, looks and constructs (and indeed, other forms of social identity) as it changes through time, the more it defines a film as subversive, silly, or both. Few horror films survive this process. What is terrifying to one generation may be amusing to another, simply because the variables of social performance have changed and either cannot continue to support their preferred reading or offer the possibility of re-negotiated or alternative readings. Some contemporary film-makers exploit the tension between horror and humour as the subject of the text (see Paul 1994). This will be explored further, but the over-arching mythic structure in which symbolic creatures play out tragic disruptions in order to insist upon the comic joy of survival is arguably the reason for the consistent presence of the genre, and its recycling of recognisable types of monster in contemporary forms.

The horror film, like the fairytale, also engages with what Bruno Bettelheim has called 'the existential predicament', where 'a struggle against severe difficulties in life is unavoidable, an intrinsic part of human existence', informing all significant rites of passage (1978: 8). While Bettelheim argues that the fairytale has an inevitably optimistic outcome, offering happy endings, the horror film remains ambivalent in this respect. What it continues to share with the fairytale, however, is the exigency of *process*. Writer and director Terry Gilliam has suggested that cinematic fairytales like horror and fantasy films need to continually construct problems for their protagonists to deal with, because it is the process that is affecting, not the outcome. As he has commented, 'I read my daughter a version of *Little Red Riding Hood* that had been so bowdlerised that the wolf had problems eating people, the huntsman didn't know what to do, and the little girl wasn't scared at all. What is the point? You have to have the horrors in order to survive them, and triumph over them'.

Historian and critic Marina Warner (1994) has further argued that this process, in being a struggle for both meaning and identity, has been important for engaging with gender issues, and especially in articulating a complex feminine voice, an idea which persists throughout the history of the horror film. Furthermore, the articulation of the female perspective has traditionally found a powerful home in gothic literature, and it is this we shall turn to now.

The gothic tradition

Gothic literature takes up the super-structure of myth and the process of fairytale and configures them in a form which is a direct reaction to the age of Enlightenment, adopting a fervently anti-rationalist stance. Horace Walpole's *Castle of Otranto* (1764) explores the nature of transgression and insists upon a relationship between the natural and the supernatural rather than drawing an obvious distinction between them. His re-configuration of the medieval romance is ultimately melodramatic and moralistic, using the paraphernalia of the gothic to create an uncertain space, charged with inadmissible and unpredictable effects. This kind of theatrical ambivalence prevails in the horror film, and is all the more affecting for being beyond the obvious realms of understanding and control.

William Beckford's *Vathek* (1786) explores hedonistic and aesthetic imperatives, and consequently challenges established ethical considerations. It explores the effect of the Oriental 'other', and the ways in which the constraints of one culture are liberated in the magical, non-social, predications of another. Although Ann Radcliffe's *The Mysteries of Udolpho* (1794) is an accomplished supernatural tale, it resorts to rational explanation and justification of events. As such it is essentially a reactionary strand of the gothic which operates in complete contrast to Matthew Lewis's *The Monk* (1796), a sustained tale of wilful self-destruction which is often sexually explicit, blasphemous, and powerfully romantic in its expression of uninhibited desire. Fred Botting (1996: 60) has suggested that:

Despite differences of historical and geographical setting, the male writers of Gothic, of a more aristocratic class position, lean towards representations of irrationality and the supernatural, exercising the privileges and freedoms conferred by gender and class position. The female writers, usually more solidly middle-class in origin, remain more concerned with the limits of eighteenth-century virtues, careful to interrogate rather than overstep the boundaries of domestic propriety which, because of their gender, were more critically maintained.

The tensions in these key novels are clear reactions to an acknowledged order, expressing feelings constrained and oppressed by social laws and practice, and addressing psychological, emotional and physical imperatives.

The liberation of these fears prompted a rich tradition of female writers in the gothic genre. Citing Ann Radcliffe, Mary Shelley, the Brontes, Charlotte Perkins Gilman, Joyce Carol Oates, Angela Carter and Lisa Tuttle, Mark Jankovich argues that 'rather than encouraging female passivity, obedience, and ignorance, many Gothic novels justified activity, disobedience, and the pursuit of knowledge on the part of their female characters' (1992: 20). Kate Ferguson Ellis affirms that these novels allowed 'the female heroine to purge the infected home and to establish a new one, by having her re-enact the disobedience of Eve, and bring out of that a new Eden "far happier"' (1989).

Angela Carter, novelist and collaborator in the film adaptation of her short story *The Company of Wolves* (1984), remarked:

The girl at the beginning of the film is a direct homage to the Hammer films. I wanted it to be a lyrical romance in the style of Powell and Pressburger. The difficulty for me is the fact that the film has been about a girl coming to terms with her libido, and yet when confronted with the pure "libido" of the wolves, she screams! She could have just smiled, that would have been all right. I also disapproved of the eighteenth-century moralité at the end. It didn't seem at all suitable. She could handle the wolf.

Ultimately, these stories become ways of examining psychological, emotional, physical, social, cultural and historical divisions, and are a forewarning of the expression of fears which divide humankind from itself. This notion of division and 'the divided soul' is best expressed in Mary Shelley's *Frankenstein* (1818), through the characters of the doctor and his creation, where in trying to re-awaken life in the dead, the doctor self-evidently transgresses the sacred and ethical codes which are accorded to human life, thus initiating not merely a complex discourse about the treatment of body and soul, but others concerning guilt, moral responsibility, and scientific and political impact.

Ken Russell's film *Gothic* (1986) camply recounts the stormy nights at the Villa Diodati in Geneva where Lord Byron, Percy Byshe Shelley, Mary Shelley and Byron's physician, William Polidori, told each other provocative ghost stories. Ultimately, one result was Mary Shelley's *Frankenstein* and another Polidori's *The Vampyre* (1819), in which the vampiric hero Ruthven is partially based on Byron. This particularly English inflection of the vampire myth is crucially important because it comes to inform many of the cinematic interpretations of the vampire, removing it from its more ancient Greek, Roman and Slavonic sources. Ken Russell's credentials in the horror genre were established by *The Devils* (1971) and extended in another Bram Stoker tale, *The Lair of the White Worm* (1988).

The motif of the divided sensibility expressed in *Frankenstein* also characterises Robert Louis Stevenson's *The Strange Case of Dr Jekyll and Mr Hyde* (1886) and Bram Stoker's *Dracula* (1897). These stories, in their various manifestations, became the primary models for the early horror films, concerning themselves with how the limits of human desire and endeavour play out within an established social and spiritual order. Arguably, these three stories, and a fourth, Conan Doyle's *The Hound of the Baskervilles* (1939) constitute not merely the dominant models in the development of Hollywood's early genre output, but structurally define much of the genre in general. *Frankenstein* establishes the scientist as a key figure, introduces a creature which plays out issues of identity and ethical conduct, and creates a narrative which operates as a template for stories addressing the crises of modernity. *Dracula* engages with ideas about European otherness, predatory threat, uninhibited expressions of sexual desire, the secular power myth of blood, and the sacred religious symbolism it challenges. *The Strange Case of Dr Jeckyll and My Hyde* plays out the tension between social identity, civilised codes of conduct, and the more primal and inchoate instincts of humanity, while *The Hound of the Baskervilles* creates a powerful, folkloric mythology to be rationalised by the most renowned detective of the era.

Often overlooked as a key influence, though, is *Melmoth the Wanderer* (1820) by Charles Maturin, which deals with the Faustian myth of a man, Melmoth, selling his soul to the Devil in exchange for prolonged life. He attempts to prolong it still further by finding someone about to die to take his place in hell. Interestingly, this requires Melmoth to visit prisons, asylums, hospitals and battlegrounds, as places where life may be imminently lost. These contexts alone further delineate the terrain of the horror text in that they move beyond the limits of duality represented in the key gothic texts, and examine the limits of law and order, aspects of madness, the destabilisation of the body, and the transience and lack of purpose in life itself. This study of abnormality and transgression, though socially grounded, still retains its ultimately mythic dimension.

In the United States, Charles Brockden Brown's equally neglected but influential *Wieland* (1798) anticipates one of the prevailing sites of American horror, the family home, in dealing with a man, driven by supernatural imperatives, to kill his wife and children. The psychological aspects of the novel are highly persuasive, and prefigure the work of Edgar Allan Poe and Nathaniel Hawthorne in rendering a world made strange by paranormal forces.

Fantasy and reality

Poe is especially effective in translating the (often comic) surreality of gothic motifs into the aberrance and obsession of mental life, externalising the deep tensions within the human sensibility into the material world. It was this that appealed to D. W. Griffith, who made a compendium of Poe's material into one of the first major horror films of the silent era in the United States, entitled *The Avenging Conscience* (1914). Based predominantly on *The Tell-Tale Heart* (1850) but including aspects of *The Black Cat* (1850) and the poem *The Bells* (1849), the film tells the story of a young man who murders his oppressive uncle because he opposes his new-found love, and walls him within the chimney breast. After watching a spider catch a fly and some ants overcome a spider, the young man concludes that life 'is a long system of murder', words which chime with some of the new Darwinian ideas that mainstream culture was becoming aware of, and which Griffith exploits for their metaphoric and alienating effects. Griffith was later to make *The Sorrows of Satan* (1926), based on Marie Corelli's modern version of the Faust myth, which Carlos Clarens admires for 'establishing the first precept of psychological horror: never show too much on the screen' (1967: 61), largely because it shows Satan's shadow overwhelming his terrified victim rather than showing a potentially risible man-in-devil-suit.

Although contemporary novels and plays provided more source materials for horror films during the silent era, the genre did not wholly establish itself as a distinctive and popular form. *A Blind Bargain* (1922), featuring Lon Chaney, and based both on Barry Pain's *The Octave of Claudius* (1900) and H. G. Wells' *The Island of Dr Moreau* (1896), as well as the pioneering work of Frenchman Alexis Carrell in the area of organ transplant, successfully engages with the workings of the 'mad scientist' and a key theme of the genre: humankind's irresistible dabbling into things which should best be left alone, in the name of a seemingly spurious spirit of progress. However, its fantastic, melodramatic quality only serves to distance itself from, rather than enhance, its potentially horrific implications and effects. It is this sense of the fantastic which undermines its persuasiveness as a text of its times, especially in the light of the predominance of what Kevin Brownlow (1990) has called the realist films of 'social conscience' which characterise the silent era.

The horror film, in being a 'fantastic' text, was by definition non-realist, and more often than not, perceived as funny. Harry Pollard's *The Devil's Assistant* (1917) is described by Brownlow: 'a skeleton on horseback gathers up the girl and rides through the night sky. A bearded boatman rows them across the Styx, where stray souls struggle in the fog-shrouded water. Cerberus, the three-headed dog, guards the gates to Hades'. Critic Wid Gunning comments: 'along with the other weird things, he had a big dog with a couple of bum heads hung on either side of his real head, and – oh boy! – if they don't get a laugh it'll be because no one in your community has a sense of humour' (cited in Brownlow 1990: 104–5).

Ironically, by attempting to use metaphor to engage with issues concerning the hallucinatory or adverse effects of drugs, the film did not sit well against more literal narratives addressing the topic. During the silent era, film demonstrated an increasingly symbiotic relationship with real-life events, often depicting interpretations of noted crimes, sex and drugs scandals and political injustice. Arguably, given the tensions that these films provoked with censors, moral advocacy groups, and the general film-going public, it became necessary for a genre to evolve which depicted issues and events in a metaphoric and less literal way. Consequently, the monster would evolve as the symbolic embodiment of the complex agendas raised in the social conscience films of the silent period. With the advent of sound, and the prominence of the musical, the comedy and the western, the horror film took its place as both spectacle and social mediator.

The lack of morality, and the degrading representations of the 'beast' in humankind, so often commented upon by critics of the crime film in the silent era could be safely literalised in the monster from afar, and was simultaneously able to distract attention from the real social ills in American life. One of the determinants of the transition and emergence of the horror film out of the silent era in the United States is the influence of the German *Expressionist** films, so key in the evolution of the genre as a whole. Brownlow notes that another drug-oriented narrative, *Human Wreckage* (1923) (written by C. Gardner Sullivan, and first entitled *The Living Dead*) depicted the psychological state of a drug addict through a set designed in a similar way to that of *The Cabinet of Dr Caligari* (1919). The distorted lines, jagged angles and fragmentary shapes are drawn directly from Expressionist design, which in the case of *Caligari* reflected madness, dream states and paranoia, and a more open, less literally determined conception of an interior state. *Caligari's* horror resides more in the design, creating an oppressive and frightening atmosphere, than in the attempt to show an 'affected' mind. Its status as a German film saw *Caligari* fall foul of protest by the highly conservative American Legion at its Los Angeles première, but it remained highly influential on the films which emerged from the Universal lot later in the 1930s. As Phil Hardy notes: 'where *Caligari* represents a style and a vision, *Frankenstein* represents a formula, and the beginnings of a genre' (1985: ix). It was a genre destined to emerge very rapidly.

The German version of gothic literature called the *Schauerromane* proved influential on the early German gothic cinema. Predicated on questioning the validity of everyday material existence, and playing out sometimes erotic and violent scenarios, these stories provided a ready texture for the expressionist and quasi-surreal cinematic narratives to follow. *The Cabinet of Dr Caligari*, *Nosferatu* and *The Golem* (1920) were early masterpieces that proved influential elsewhere, largely because as well as chiming with the dominant models of the monster (the madman, the un-dead, the man-made creature, the vampire) they progressed aspects of cinema itself and were motivated by an artistic seriousness that was soon to dissipate in the Hollywood model. Using mirrors, shadows, stark contrasts in design, costume and location, and a range of visual effects, the films envisaged and illustrated interior states and supernatural vistas. This emphasis prioritised abstraction over narrative and addressed the precarious nature of human sanity in a world of complex power relations and unknown forces. Studies in obsession revealed a fine line between utopian desire and dystopian inevitability. As the individual conspired to achieve power and control the forces of nature, the urban oppression of the modern era compromised these ambitions. To rise above these obstacles, however, was to know both the terror and tranquillity of the sublime. This was also a key theme of German Romantic thought, and later an implicit ideological tenet of National Socialism.

The complex relationship between German art and politics has not diluted the importance of the key German Expressionist films of the silent era, nor that of the emigré directors F. W. Murnau, Fritz Lang, and Paul Leni in influencing the style of the Hollywood horror movie, if not its content (see Kracauer 1947; Eisner 1973; Walker 1978; Salt 1979; Prawer 1980; Petrie 1985). The horrors of real executions seen in arcade peep-show machines, the depictions of disease and poverty in films like *The Toll of Mammon* (1914), the threatening otherness of the supposedly violent and malevolent Chinese, and the highly politicised agendas of films relating to working conditions, were all key thematics in the silent-era social conscience films. These were to be submerged, along with the German Expressionist motifs, into the new gothic at a time when nation-wide processes of 'Americanisation' were re-determining and advancing the dominant myths of frontier culture, democracy and patriotism. Monsters could be foreign, define the process of death and decay, stand outside the law and threaten civilised principles, but crucially were not American either by birth, or perhaps more importantly, in spirit.

In a key transitional period *The Phantom of the Opera* (1925), again featuring Lon Chaney, took $10,000 a week in box office receipts and fully established the genre as a viable commercial and artistic endeavour, playing out subterranean or supernatural threats against a quasi-bourgeois status quo, a consistent theme of the genre. Thus, by re-contextualising issues in the metaphors of fairytale horror, they could be both addressed and resolved, something not possible in the silent realist narratives, in which often the only resolution was that the principle figures died.

Browning and beyond

By directing five key films between 1927 and 1936, Tod Browning became a significant figure in defining the horror film in the United States. *London After Midnight* (1927), *Dracula* (1931), *Freaks* (1932), *Mark of the Vampire* (1935) and *The Devil Doll* (1936) all serve to engage with the monster in a way that demonstrates what Stuart Rosenthal has described as 'situations of moral and sexual frustration' (1975: 9). Arguably, the explicit nature of these issues in the 'social conscience' films are contained within the generic constraints of the horror film, but create huge tensions in the ways

45

that these limits are tested. Browning's own sexuality may underpin his obsessional interest with the attraction and repulsion of sub-human figures, whether they are mythic creatures like the vampire or deformed human beings. Browning defines the monster within a model of animality, and constantly poses the question of what it is to be human. It is this potentially sentimentalised conception of the monster which also characterises James Whale's version of *Frankenstein* (1931), calling upon the audience to sympathise with Boris Karloff's creature, as well as to feel uneasy and threatened in its presence. In effect both Browning and Whale motivate their monsters; many of the key figures here merely wish to understand their own monstrosity in the eyes of others, and it is only when they are further alienated do they seek revenge, and use their otherness in a spirit of aggression.

In many senses, these horror films are concerned with the limits of control, and lead readily to a whole range of texts in which science, as the supposed mediator of order and rationality, becomes the instrument of chaos in hands that seek to play out more extreme codes of conduct (see, for example, Tudor 1989). Incidentally, James Whale and his less notable, but influential, directorial colleague Ed Wood Jnr are celebrated in film biographies: *Gods and Monsters* (1998) and *Ed Wood* (1994), which prove to be exemplars of the increasing recognition of the influence of the horror genre on mainstream film-making. Both men project complex aspects of their sexuality and relationship to class into their films. The increasing amount of self-reflexive knowledge about such figures among fans also ensures a popular audience for the movies. Tim Burton, director of *Ed Wood,* plays out these early genre influences in a number of his works, most notably Browning's *Freaks* in *Batman Returns* (1992), Whale's *Frankenstein* in *Edward Scissorhands* (1990), and Jules Bass's animated *Mad Monster Party* (1968) in *The Nightmare Before Christmas* (1993).

Whale, Browning, and later Paul Leni, consistently address notions of social facade, the damaging sexual inhibitions of civilised codes of practice, and the guilt and anxiety in not being able to adjust to social orthodoxies. However, the intensity of these thematic interests is often undercut by the melodramatic and sometimes comic thrust of both performance and narrative outcome. *Freaks* (see Russo 1994) and *Dracula*, however, remain persuasive in having a sense of unease which permeates each scene, and represent the sheer 'difference' being shown on screen. The monster is threatening by virtue of its otherness, but more so by its *proximity* to humanity. Essentially, this sense of humanity-at-one-remove is a displacement of anxiety, and a ready context for the social ills of 1920s and 1930s America to be simultaneously forgotten or attributed to other contexts. Although *Freaks* is essentially about physiological and psychiatric disorder, and *Dracula* is an invocation of the supernatural, many horror films of the 1930s demonstrated a particular concern with science and its centrality in the context of social progress, a mantle that was to grow through its dark post-war zenith with the atomic bomb to its naturalised place within the new suburban utopias of the 1950s. However, during the 1930s the presence of the 'mad scientist' was invariably concerned either with a seemingly necessary visionary eccentricity that risked all for the sake of progress, or merely megalomaniac ambition that resulted in damaging outcomes and wrong-doing.

Henry Frankenstein (Colin Clive), in Whale's 1931 classic, poses an important question: 'Where should we be if nobody tried to find out what lies beyond?' continuing, 'Have you never wanted to look beyond the clouds and stars, to know what causes trees to bud and what changes darkness into light?' before adding, 'But if you talk like that people call you crazy'. Frankenstein's curiosity extends beyond finding out the laws of nature, however, and becomes an aspiration to create his own law. It is in this transgression (the act of trying to create a human figure in his own image) that Frankenstein violates not merely scientific convention but the work of God. This profanity has a more public agenda, posing ethical rather than scientific questions. When Dr Von Niemann (Lionel Atwill) in *The Vampire Bat* (1933) creates life, even his own assistant fails to believe that this is in the name of progress, and shoots his mentor. It seems the horror of such narratives lies in witnessing the violation of humanity's limits and the sense of the humane. An implied consensus of decorum has been transgressed, and the symbolic consequences of the transgression commands sympathy in the audience because the monster is only a materialisation of an unnatural and unwanted order. The monster is essentially a physical manifestation of the consequences of misconduct.

There is a sense, however, that the mad scientists are also magicians, and that science is an accident of their imaginative actions. Their key imperative is an avoidance of the 'everyday' and its inhibiting values. The willingness of the mad scientist to transcend the laws of nature has a parallel desire in wanting to break social limitations. Robert Louis Stevenson's *The Strange Case of Dr Jeckyll and Mr Hyde* (1886) is as much about hypocrisy as it is about the dialectic between mind and body. However, Rouben Mamoulian's 1931 film version concentrates on delineating and exposing the sensual and sexual aspects implied in the original novella. When Dr Jeckyll (Frederic March) confronts his fiance Muriel (Rose Hobart) he says: 'I was drawn to the mysteries of science, to the unknown. But now the unknown wears your face, looks back at me with your eyes'. Jeckyll's main imperative then becomes one of cleansing himself by separating his two natures. Science becomes the instrument of liberation, not merely in the grandiose sense of progress, but also in the redemption of the personal and private when it risks becoming public. Mr Hyde, like Frankenstein's monster, becomes this public persona, but as Tom Milne has noted, this is not about the embodiment of monstrous and perverse excesses, but 'the frustration by society of his own perfectly natural, unorgiastic desires' (1969: 39). Again, consensual norms seemingly misrepresent humankind, and outside the context of the social conscience film, the monster represents what is ultimately a comment upon the limitations of the moral and cultural infrastructure, without seeming to transgress social norms or generic expectations.

Sometimes science is genuinely threatening, however, and in *The Invisible Ray* (1936), featuring Boris Karloff, 'Radium X' destroys its maker, making a salient comment about the possible effects of nuclear power long before its prominence in the 'creature features' of the 1950s. In these kind of horror films, the mad scientist in many ways becomes a symbol for patterns of change which are somehow inappropriate or out of control. The monster is the anachronism of certain tools and technologies in the wrong hands at the wrong time. The true horror lies in the fact that these things cannot be un-invented, and that their impacts are inevitable, merely awaiting the context that global confrontation was later to provide.

Sadism and sequels

As Universal Studios consolidated its position in developing and essentially constructing the paraphernalia of the horror genre, its codes and conventions became increasingly apparent. It was necessary to create sequels, and to ensure that the terrors played out in horror films were sufficiently petrifying but acceptably conservative. *The Bride of Franken-stein* (1935), with its prologue re-visiting the Villa Diodati, encouraging Mary Shelley (Elsa Lanchester) to 'tell us another one', engenders yet further sympathy for Karloff's creature, and ultimately plays out as a witty comedy of manners in which Dr Praetorius (Ernest Thesinger) is a megalomaniac version of the mad scientist. While Praetorius remains a manipulative and threatening figure, some of the horrors cut from the final film (a series of brutal murders by his assistant Karl, and a live dissection of a woman with catalepsy) are an indication of the fine line between terror effects and unacceptable depictions of sadism. Early prints of *Frankenstein* had been cut, removing the scene in which the creature accidentally murders a little girl, but which had the outcome, as Leslie Halliwell observes, that the audience 'assume the monster must have raped her' (1988: 122). Tensions between suggestion and the overt representation of brutalities enjoyed by those who commit them were to continue to characterise films of the 1930s and to test the censors.

The National Board of Censorship of Motion Pictures, later the National Board of Review, was set up to monitor Hollywood movies in 1908. The excesses and scandals of the Hollywood community prompted an increasingly vigilant eye on its product. In order to counteract the possibility of State intervention, the film industry itself formed the Motion Pictures Producers and Distributors of America (MPPDA), headed by William Hays, to monitor its conduct, lobby to re-assure Federal arbitrators and provide guidelines for the studios. A production code was later formulated and regulated by the Hays Office, senior Hollywood producers and the Board of the MPPDA. The work of the Hays Office became increasingly censorious under Joseph Breen after 1934, and the impacts and effects of film classification and censorship still provoke contentious debates. The British Board of Film Censors was formed in 1913; one of its most significant contributions was to ban the production, distribution, exhibition and import of horror movies during the Second World War.

The key models of the horror film were being formulated to test the limits of representation. Whale's *The Old Dark House* (1932) combines black comedy with shock effects in a way that anticipates many later examples. *White Zombie* (1932), echoing Carl Dreyer's *Vampyr* (1932), co-opts the dream-like and poetic into a troubling and surreal narrative, the first to properly engage with the un-dead 'zombie' as a metaphor, here a nod to Depression conformity and exploitation; later, for example, in George Romero's *Night of the Living Dead*, the return of dead Americans chiming with the losses in Vietnam. *The Mask of Fu Manchu* (1932), *The Hands of Orlac* (1935) and most notably, *The Hounds of Zaroff* (1932) all play out almost fetishistic and ritualised models of sadistic extremism, the latter implying the fascistic undertow of European decadence (that was later evidenced in Hitler, Mussolini, and Stalin) in the figure of Count Zaroff (Leslie Banks). The sense of European otherness is palpable in these characters, and although indicative of American isolationist fears, is actually more bound up with distancing cruel rationality and self-indulgence from the more preferable American folk-cultures and urbane wit evidenced in populist texts of the same period.

Hollywood had responded to the poverty and hardship of the Depression by largely ignoring it, producing instead a range of escapist and utopian entertainments which served as distractions from social malaise. Busby Berkeley musicals like *42nd Street* (1933) and *The Gold Diggers of 1933* (1933) prioritised spectacle and showcased energy and endeavour through the metaphor of a creative community creating utopian entertainments. RKO's musicals featured the elegance and sophistication of Fred Astaire and Ginger Rogers, and foregrounded dancing as the embodiment of liberation and the fulfilment of romantic passion. Frank Capra's populist comedies *It Happened One Night* (1934), *Mr Deeds Goes* to Town (1936), *Lost Horizon* (1937) and *Mr Smith Goes to Washington* (1939) extolled the virtues of small town America and the common decency of the homely and hard-working hero driven by the self-evident truths of the Constitution and the pioneering achievements of the American forefathers. The State and its systems were represented as the epitome of democratic process and were spoiled only by corrupt individuals, who could be brought to justice. This utopian idyll was best epitomised in the animated films of the Walt Disney Studios – 'Disney' has in many senses become an ideological brand name for a particular value system predicated on populist principles. Mapped against these texts, the horror film was a pertinent and persuasive model of the darker underbelly of American culture.

While Frankenstein got a son (*Son of Frankenstein* (1939)) and Dracula a daughter (*Dracula's Daughter* (1936)) in persuasive sequels (the latter, for example, enjoying a strong lesbian undercurrent), the most enduring monster proved to be *King Kong* (1933). Effectively a re-telling of *Beauty and the Beast*, the film embodies many of the key themes of the genre: the ambivalence of the monster, the metaphoric implications of Kong's (black) masculinity and sexuality, the consequences of imperialist intervention and exploitation, the limits of exploration and endeavour, and the predilection for confrontation and irrationality. *King Kong* is a mythic compendium of Depression-era anxieties, borrowing much from fairytale, and insisting that much that is frightening about horror films is intrinsically bound up with how texts question the maintenance of social norms while allowing the most intense feelings experienced by humankind to find an appropriate context. Fears are not merely expressed through brutality but through a sentimental apocalypse which both acknowledges consensus and constraint and simultaneously reveals *how it is possible* to feel. It is this which remains disturbing in films of this period. As Basil Wright has observed, 'in their doomed pursuits of beauty and happiness, the movie monsters ... reflected something of the despair of the Depression years' (cited in Lloyd 1983: 55). Even in the 1990s, when the Universal and RKO horrors were often dismissed as camp, David Cronenberg has suggested, 'Films like *Frankenstein*, *Dracula* and *King*

Kong in now being understood as 'camp' can show the truth about 'feeling' in a way that camp performance actually reveals'.

It is pertinent to end this section with reference to *The Black Cat* (1934). Hjalmar Poelzig (Boris Karloff), an architect responsible for war crimes, has built an almost Bauhaus-style mansion over the graveyard of the First World War dead. Part mausoleum, part exhibition, the mansion houses Poelzig's dead wife embalmed in a glass case. Dr Vitus Werdegast (Bela Lugosi) returns from fifteen years in a Russian prison to take revenge on Poelzig, who was responsible for his imprisonment, and who, we learn, married Werdegast's wife and later Werdegast's daughter. This revenge plot is merely a vehicle by which the bigger issue of the moral, ethical and social tragedy of the First World War is addressed. Poelzig, dismissing Werdegast's desire for revenge as an almost petty act in the face of the actual and deep spiritual losses of the past, argues 'Are we not both the living dead?', suggesting that humankind has not understood the nature of death, nor the preciousness and precariousness of life. The true horror lies in humankind's refusal to take responsibility for its past, and the feeling of guilt this creates is played out in the perverse preservation and amoral violence at the mansion. *The Black Cat* promotes a modernist agenda through gothic motifs and successfully invokes the sacred, the profane, and a troubling secularism, all wholly attuned to the changing social model, rendering the horrors of the past as at best forewarnings of new terrors and at worst fantastic clichés. The achievements of the horror film in the 1930s were soon matters for nostalgia, however, with the rise of National Socialism, and the beginning of the Second World War.

Revival and survival

The re-issue of a double bill of *Frankenstein* and *Dracula* in 1937 to world-wide markets proved commercially successful and defined the dominant paradigms of the genre, which still remain prominent whenever the genre needs to rejuvenate or re-invent itself. Significantly, the sense of revival soon became generic survival in the light of the impact of World War Two. An important Middle-European market had been lost, and it was uniformly assumed that horror films were inappropriate in the light of the real horrors of warfare (see Halliwell 1988). In essence, the monsters of the 1930s became comic figures, but as was often noted in the focus groups interviewed about these films, the monster movies of the 1940s, particularly the comedies which allied the Universal monsters with comedians like Abbott and Costello, afforded an opportunity for a younger audience to see the famous monsters on screen for the first time. In 1943, when *Frankenstein Meets the Wolf Man* was released to great box office success, the reflexivity and parodic aspects of the horror canon were clearly acknowledged. This was one of the first examples of revising not merely the dominant narratives of the genre, but also the cinematic codes and conventions that had been established in relation to those narratives in Hollywood.

With Karloff and Lugosi often reduced to caricature, new monsters like the Wolf Man and the Mummy merely repeating old scenarios, horror motifs being played out self-consciously and melodramatically, and horror movies made explicitly as comedies, the genre was at a crossroads. The fine line between suspense used for the purposes of fright and the instigation of comic 'pay-off' was noticeably breached when the audience was encouraged to laugh at the fear of others (Lou Costello, for example) rather than empathise with the threat towards, or the context actually experienced by, the victim. As Stephen King has noted:

They're very close, humour and horror. Those of us who are involved with doing one or the other prove our essential childishness because we have to have instant gratification. They're the only two genres I know that cause an audience to make an audible reaction. You know at once whether you've succeeded or not. You can be in the lobby of a theatre and hear sounds coming from the auditorium. You know they're either screaming or laughing, so its either a good comedy or a good horror picture. As far as I know the only difference is it starts being horror and stops being humour when it stops being somebody else and starts being you.

King's point is pertinent, recognising how horror and humour can turn upon the viewer's identification with the terror. If the viewer empathises with the subject or victim then it is likely that the fright will be mutually experienced. Distance from the victim's experience, however, will facilitate an objectivity which creates a different kind of viewing pleasure; either one which enables laughter at another's misfortune, or promotes a potentially critical understanding of the mechanism by which the protagonist is being victimised. Crucially, this changes the perspective by which violent acts and death may be understood. Satiric illustrator and authorial inspiration for the television and film versions of *The Addams Family*, Charles Addams, notes, 'I want to make death as pleasant as possible, especially for myself. I think of it as a rather cosy condition that shouldn't be too upsetting. It comes to us all so we might as well joke about it. As long as we can laugh at it I think we're that much ahead'. Such perspectives are a long way from the mournfulness of *The Black Cat*, and demonstrate how far humour attempts to deconstruct and dilute the *actual* nature of death, resisting its finality, and encouraging a more comforting security to the notion of an 'end'. The horror film of the 1940s is therefore an ambiguous tool, drawing attention to horror but dissipating its effects. Concurrently, it acknowledges the war, but displaces its outcomes.

In the most persuasive horror texts of the 1940s, however, displacement is used not to distanciate from threat, but to heighten it through suggestion. The psychological horror produced by Val Lewton, and directed by Jacques Tourneur, Mark Robson and Robert Wise at RKO Studios, returned to the fairytale archetypes of old world myth and superstition to engage with what Wise has called 'the dramatisation of the threat of the unknown'. In many senses, the 'modernity' of psychoanalysis was being brought to bear on the paraphernalia of the supernatural legend. Lon Chaney Jnr, who had effectively established himself as the next movie monster star after Karloff and Lugosi, argued that he had won the sympathy of the audience because his monsters were extreme variations on physical ugliness, mean-spiritedness and ignorance – all essentially 'known' quantities. Lewton's films were a recourse to the partially known but unexplored presence and influence of a folkloric order. In operating as part of a mythic past, these narrative subjects had accrued taboo status by harbouring hidden knowledges that the modern world was ill-prepared to accept and needed to absorb or repress.

Waiting for the bus

Poet, novelist, MGM publicist, and sociologist of 1930s America, Val Lewton, brought a literary and cultural breath to the $150,000, 75-minute 'B' pictures he and his associates made during the 1940s. Working within these limits (and the imposition of a market-tested title) Lewton rejuvenated the horror genre. He returned to a 'people-centred' approach, and the de-familiarisation of European sources, in order to counter the prominence of monsters, who were once foreign but now hugely Americanised by audience over-familiarity. *Cat People* (1942), inspired by a dream and the recollection of brutal Russian folk-tales (see Siegel 1972) features Balkan-born designer Irena Dubrovna (Simone Simon), who is descended from a race of 'catpeople', transforming into a panther when aroused by masculine intimidation and sexual jealousy. In the film this is implied and illustrated through key scenes; for example at a dimly-lit swimming pool, where Alice (Jane Randolph) is menaced by an unseen beast. Lewton named these specific sequences 'buses', on the basis of another scene in the film where the suspense created when Alice is followed by another unseen presence is alleviated by the release of the pressure brakes on a passing bus.

Lewton's approach, although highly distinctive, became increasingly formulaic in the series of horror films he made at RKO studios. As he suggests, 'No grisly stuff for us. No mask-like faces hardly human, with gnashing teeth and hair standing on end. No creaking manifestations. No horror piled on horror. You can't keep up a horror that's long sustained. It becomes something to laugh at' (cited in Siegel 1972: 31). This perspective underpins the ways in which the Universal chillers of the 1940s were perceived, and later became, so much so that in *Cat People*, Lewton mocks the Universal canon when Alice warns Dr Judd (Tom Conway) that he should not visit Irena alone: 'You want me to take some means of protection', he jokes, adding 'a gun, perhaps, with a silver bullet'. Ironically, Lewton was using the same kind of myth and superstition in his own work, but treating it with a great deal more subtlety and suggestion; for example, voodoo in *I Walked with a Zombie* (1943), primal obsession in *The Leopard Man* (1943), diabolism and witchcraft in *The Seventh Victim* (1943), the otherness of the repressed child in *Curse of the Catpeople* (1944), folkloric vampires and the plague in *Isle of the Dead* (1945), grave-robbing in the cause of science in *The Body Snatcher* (1945) and madness in *Bedlam* (1946).

The last three of these films featured Boris Karloff, who subordinated his Universal persona to Lewton's more naturalistic style, and in so doing demonstrated the shift of emphasis that had occurred in the 1940s. Producer Jack Gross had also joined the RKO team from Universal, but his idea of horror as 'a werewolf chasing a girl in a night gown up a tree' (cited in Siegel 1972: 71) was fiercely resisted. Lewton effectively modified the notion of transformation in the horror film into a psychological and emotional act that recalled primal imperatives. Further, he played out a variety of perspectives on 'reason' which were largely inadequate or ill-conceived in the light of unknown forces. By reducing the physical monstrosity of the Universal films, and stimulating the audience to induce their own terror, Lewton's work does much to parallel, invoke, and implicitly illustrate the unimaginable terrors of the Second World War. The sense of darkness and doom is rarely relieved in Lewton's films, which confront death in ways which remain sensitive to its actual presence in a variety of global contexts.

Post-war perils

The 1950s horror films effectively play out important tensions in the post-war period, anticipating the changing styles and cultures of the following decade. In the United States, the rise of the 'Creature Feature', engaging with post-Atomic Bomb anxiety, the Cold War fear of communist infiltration, and the internal contradictions of a new American identity, was paralleled by a persistence of the gothic in the rise of the Hammer studios in England. Comic ambivalence persisted in the gimmickry associated with the films of William Castle.

Castle was the director of *The House on the Haunted Hill*, *Macabre* (1958) and *The Tingler* (1959). The latter featured an organism growing in the human spine, nourished and nurtured by fear, assuaged by the act of screaming, and also contained one of cinema's first representations of an LSD trip. Castle will be best remembered for the gimmicks he used in support of his films. One of the focus groups had fond memories of 'Emergo', the skeleton that seemed to emerge from the screen during *The House on the Haunted Hill*. Castle's screenwriter, Robb White also has vivid recollections of these events; most notably, children 'shooting' at the skeleton with assorted pocket debris. He also remembers the night when 'Percepto', the gimmick supporting *The Tingler*, where small motors were placed on the bottoms of theatre seats to give members of the audience a brief 'tingle', accidentally went off during *The Nun's Story* (see Weaver 1991; Vale and Juno 1986).

Inevitably, however, a new realism also underpinned aspects of the horror text, as the social and cultural effects of the war determined changes in the conduct of everyday life. Transformation is a prevailing and key theme in these texts, and once more constitutes a re-configuration of the monster. Notions of consensus and constraint were changing: previous models of existence and experience were being challenged and re-defined, and with them, the horror film. Post-war anxiety can be noted in a number of cinematic models; firstly, in the rise of film noir. Film noir, a term coined by cineaste Nino Frank in 1946, from Marcel Duhamel's famous 'serie noire' book series, should be understood as a critical category and not a production category like the western or musical. Established from a range of sources: German Expressionist Cinema, French Poetic Realism, the gangster film, the hard-boiled novel, and the war-time documentary, film noir caught the spirit of post-war disillusion and featured alienated, lonely, 'non-heroic' heroes and seductive, often manipulative *femme fatales*. In a distinctive, shadowy, often downbeat style, the film noir plays out issues of existential choice in an often self-evidently meaningless and paranoid environment. This is the human condition sacrificed to an inevitable doom, leavened only by chance moments of fortune and passionate encounters.

Secondly, rapid decline may also be measured in the erstwhile utopian MGM musical, best exemplified by the work of Busby Berkeley in the 1930s and the films featuring Gene Kelly and Judy Garland in the 1940s and 1950s. These films provided a focus for, and an illustration of, utopian principles, optimism, and the expression of joy. The sheer colour, spectacle and excess in the musical suggested a sense of inevitable fulfilment. The darker aspects of American culture – the Korean War, McCarthyism, juvenile delinquency, television, and the new commerce rendered the undiluted positivity of the musical at best naive and at worst redundant. This is exemplified by the changing tenor of *On the Town* (1949) and its ostensible sequel *It's Always Fair Weather* (1955), where the unbridled energy of three sailors on shore leave in the first movie becomes jaundiced and cynical in the second. 'Once I had a dream' sings Kelly, 'but where is that dream? Up in smoke ...'. It is only a little further to the 'I could have been a contender' speech performed by Marlon Brando in *On the Waterfront* (1954). He, of course, merely gets 'a one way ticket to Palookaville'.

Thirdly, post-war change may be seen in the emergence of youth-oriented films. Significant shifts in personal, cultural and national identity, particularly in relation to gender, class and generation (race and ethnicity was to become a crucial factor later) began to re-determine the social order, fragmenting previously established models of community and simultaneously provoking a rearguard re-entrenchment in the institutional apparatus. Consequently, particularly in the United States, horror texts were constantly addressing how individualism was re-constituted in relation to the rise of key social groupings, which emerged as the determining arbitrators of societal frameworks as a consequence of post-war reconstruction. In effect, the monster in all of these texts is a metaphor of resistance, posing questions and challenges to the newly emerging social paradigms.

Us and them

In a climate of increased materialism, the enhancement of middle-class standing and values, and the escalation of large corporations, a commercial and bureaucratic ethos underpinned post-war recovery (see Biskind 1983; Jankovich 1996). The 'individual' was newly configured; now part of a model of scientific and technological progress and a corporate state which predicated a utopian ideology upon a paternalist, quasi-fundamentalist, consumer-oriented framework. The prevailing anxieties about communism, widespread poverty, and racial tension undermined this 'comfort' ethos. These were the pre-occupations of a nation increasingly divided in outlook, unable to fully comprehend the implications, on the one hand, of the use of the Atomic Bomb, and on the other, of the new freedoms of a post-war social mobility that it had afforded. In essence, the United States had created its own monsters, and needed to understand them.

The following table offers a simplistic overview of the new political cultures of 'Us and Them' which came to characterise 1950s America, and which the 'Creature Features' of this period readily engaged with: 'Us' – the Conservative and Liberal forces of democracy – pitched against 'Them' – the Communist infiltrators, and radical extremists, often in the guise of mad scientists or social 'loose cannons'. Crucially, however, it is the tensions between the conservative and liberal tendencies which are most explored in what Mark Jancovich (1996) describes as 'invasion narratives' and 'outsider narratives' in the 1950s. The relationship between the conservative and liberal agendas as they mobilised against the tides of extremism effectively delineates many of the positions available to the individual in society, and articulates aspects of the 'monstrous'. The alien, the unknown force, is a stimulus for, a symbol of, or an outcome in relation to, an interrogation of these political tensions.

In *The Thing from Another World* (1951) the presence of a 'bi-pedal, vampiric, vegetable', the (communist) threat, interestingly invokes the *liberal* tendencies of the military group, the *conservatism* in the state-supported scientist Dr Carrington (Robert Cornthwaite) and *radicalism* in

US		THEM	
CONSERVATISM	*LIBERALISM*	*COMMUNISM*	*RADICALISM*
Right-wing	Centrist	Marxist	Leftist-tendency
Authoritarian	Pluralist	Authoritarian	Pro-Individual
Interventionist	Consensual	Oppressive	Challenging
Elitist/Expert	Communal	Autocratic	Non-conformist
God-Blessed	God-Fearing	Godless	Sceptical
Military/Law	Science/Therapy	Primitive/Other	'Enemy Within'

TABLE 1 *Us and Them*

the form of scientist Nikki Nicholson (Margaret Sheridan), who challenges traditional gender roles. The film effectively plays out the plurality of political stances through the responses to the alien, and although the alien is ultimately destroyed, the process towards its destruction demonstrates the ambivalence in American society towards authoritarian certainty, consensual improvisation, and the impact of different social-cultural identities. Rather than being ultimately conservative, the film is a treatise on political instability.

The Day the Earth Stood Still (1951), a thinly-veiled metaphor for the Christ story, but played out in more fiercely conservative terms, offers the alien (Michael Rennie) and his robot sidekick, Gort, as rectifying, unifying and corrective figures for the ills of humankind. However, the over-determination of this position underlines the lack of reconciliation possible between the dominant social and political groupings cited earlier, and heightens the instability inherent in a society no longer predicated on consent and constraint. *The Beast from 20,000 Fathoms* (1953) inaugurated the cycle of 're-awakening' primitive monster films. Further examples are *The Creature from the Black Lagoon* (1954) and its sequels, *Revenge of the Creature* (1955) and *The Creature Walks Among Us* (1956), Toho Studio's *Godzilla* (1954), Roger Corman's *Monster from the Ocean Floor* (1954), *It Came From Beneath the Sea* (1955), featuring stop-motion animation by Ray Harryhausen, and *Behemoth, the Sea Monster* (1959), with work by Harryhausen's mentor, Willis O'Brien, the creator of *King Kong*.

Ray Harryhausen's work is one of the distinctive aspects of the 1950s Creature Feature cycle. His stop-motion animation was crucial in the creation of plausible prehistoric monsters, instrumental in the destruction of apparently 'real' landmarks; most notably, the giant octopus that pulls down San Francisco's Golden Gate Bridge in *It Came from Beneath the Sea*. This plot-line was initially resisted by the San Francisco Authorities on the basis that it would undermine public confidence about the safety of the bridge. Harryhausen also flew a flying saucer into Washington DC in *Earth vs the Flying Saucers* (1956). These films may be read as narratives confirming the dreadful consequences of atomic power or as the literal representation of the primordial world as it underpins the contemporary natural order. Such narratives engage with the knowledge that humankind was preceded by creatures who used the earth as a different kind of habitat, and that the place where men and women now live is one huge burial ground, an environment that science has only partially come to know and understand.

This historical anxiety is constantly re-visited. As recently as Steven Spielberg's *Jurassic Park* (1993), the primal fear of the primordial monster is again played out. *Godzilla* (1997) followed in its giant footsteps. The non-human becomes a crucial factor in determining what human values are, and once more the political context becomes vitally important. As Jonathan Lake Crane has noted, specifically with reference to *Them!* (1954), the tale of giant ants: 'Horror could no longer be considered a local phenomenon. Its depiction as a relatively isolated, geographically contained outbreak of evil or menace was a thing of the past' (1994: 121). The monster had, at least temporarily, become the macrocosm rather than a microcosm.

Republican president and World War Two military hero General Eisenhower presided over a government which ultimately sought to appease liberals and conservatives at a time when the Korean war, McCarthyism, and the emergent Civil Rights movement threatened to de-stabilise political and cultural life. Having looked so far 'inward' during the HUAC (House on Un-American Activities Committee) investigations, and feeling the inertia of stalemated foreign policies in Korea when looking 'outward', the American people needed a fresh definition of what it was to be American. As well as drawing on this political perspective, the science fiction and horror films of the period therefore consider other possibilities. Following the Roswell incident in 1947, and numerous reported sightings of UFOs in the early 1950s, the possibility of *actual* alien invasion had entered the *zeitgeist*, and was read as a discomforting element in American post-war recovery. In *Earth vs the Flying Saucers*, it is suggested that 'If they land in our nation's capital uninvited, we won't meet them with tea and cookies'. Stephen King remembers the film vividly 'because a guy made an announcement that Russia had launched the space satellite, *Sputnik*. We all felt a little disappointed because we figured only the Americans did that sort of thing. Somehow it made us feel a little bit more scared of the aliens than we might have done. Their technology might be a little better than ours'.

The Atomic Bomb was viewed not merely an agent of destruction, but also as a beacon to the Universe of an advanced technological society. In essence, if the monsters of the 1930s and 1940s were mythic, European, and of an 'old world' order, subject only to isolationist rejection, then the 1950s alien can be construed as future-oriented, unknown, and modern; often accidentally, but necessarily, invited into the agencies of American progress. This horror, although unwelcome, was inevitable, and would have profound consequences.

Size does matter

Reading the monster metaphors of 1950s horror films as tracts concerned with the nuclear threat, communist infiltration, or other political tensions, however, ignores other more mundane issues; most specifically, 'the systematic destabilisation of movie-made masculinity' (Wells 1993: 181). Films as diverse as *The Thing from Another World* (1951), *Them!* (1954), *Creature from the Black Lagoon* (1954), *Invasion of the Body Snatchers* (1956), *The Incredible Shrinking Man* (1957), *I Married a Monster From Outer Space* (1958) and *Attack of the Fifty Foot Woman* (1958), as well as articulating the deep-rooted paranoia of a politicised otherness, all address the crisis in gender relations, the re-configuration of masculinity and femininity, and anxiety about the 'natural' environment.

If the destruction of the alien is an exercise in establishing whether 'our weapons are big enough', it is clear that there is deep ambivalence in the horror texts of 1950s America about the previous assumptions of phallic power, and the orthodoxies of male and female behaviour. Men 'shrink' while women 'rise'; taken-for-granted and insignificant aspects of the domestic environment, like ants and spiders, or cats and dogs, grow in proportion and threaten the natural order; different models of sexuality begin to threaten heterosexual and patriarchal norms. Effectively, the monsters help to delineate the limits of what it is to be a man, and accelerate the redefinition of the status and position of women.

Otherness in the alien can in some ways be allied to the *difference* inherent in women, or indeed other paradigms of sexuality, which in turn provoke changes in the male protagonists. In alien take-over movies like *Invasion of the Body Snatchers*, 'to be 'taken-over' is not so much about being absorbed by another, more dominant, ideology, as about being given new psychic and physical space in which to address difference and address fresh alternatives' (Wells 1993: 197). Consequently, what was previously 'inhuman' becomes a metaphor for potentially radical imperatives. This radicalism in sex and sexuality was addressed in different ways, especially within the English context of the Hammer horror film and its re-working of the gothic.

Fangs in Kate O'Mara's cleavage

The Hammer studios reworked the gothic stories of *Frankenstein* and *Dracula* in the late-1950s and the 1960s, making full use of lurid colour and heightened sexual tension. Seen in the full light of the post-Ealing period, the sustained snigger of the *Carry On* films and the earnestness of 'kitchen sink' realism, Hammer's horrors played out a *Grand Guignol** version of the now standardised monster motifs, using British actors from the costume tradition and the model of restrained gothic melodrama that had previously served the Universal pictures so well. Grand Guignol was a style of French theatre in which horror was explicitly dramatised through the use of blood effects and overt (if melodramatic) acts of violence.

Initially located in the *Théâtre de Grand Guignol*, a de-consecrated church in the Pigalle district of Paris in 1897, and presented by police officer and gallows assistant Oscar Métènier, the plays concentrated on the madness and psychoses of real people and not overt 'monsters'. This naturalism necessitated that everyday objects and events, like telephones and telephone calls, become part of the implied threat. Much has been borrowed from the genre; most notably its bloody effects, the imminence and randomness of death and its erotic undercurrents, but the theatrical horror faded in the pre-war period when the genre was embraced by the Nazis, and further, when the real atrocities of war proved a greater horror than the bloody eye-gougings and stranglings expected in the plays themselves.

Hammer adapted Guignol trappings and soon became Britain's greatest 'exploitation' studio, gradually increasing the violent and bloody excesses in the films as well as including nudity and the implication of perverse sexual encounters. Exploitation cinema may be understood as any (usually cheaply made) film which seeks to exploit a current trend or phenomenon for ostensibly commercial rather than artistic imperatives. This is achieved by including titillatory and often taboo elements such as gratuitous nudity, sexual acts, graphic depictions of violence, and 'anti-social' or 'gross' activities (vomiting, defecating and so on). In the postmodern era many such films have found appreciation from scholars and critics who identify a potentially subversive or radical aesthetic in their narratives. Some have also argued that these films often provide a template for bigger mainstream productions.

Encouraged by the success of Hammer's nuclear-conscious *Curse of Frankenstein* (1957) and the rehabilitation of the genre on television, with the revival of the Universal horror movies in syndication, exploitation film-makers like Gramercy Pictures and American International Productions (AIP) were prolific in adding titles to the trend. Gramercy's *The Monster That Challenged the World* (1956), *The Vampire* (1957) and *The Return of Dracula* (1958) demonstrate the creative juxtaposition between the pragmatism of making a film inexpensively, and engaging with mythic yet archetypal themes. Producer Arnold Laven notes, 'the richest, most visual, effective sequences production-wise, were those that were shot outdoors, where even a low-budget film is in a sense on equal standing with the most high-budgeted pictures', while screenwriter Patricia Fielder stresses that for *The Vampire*, 'the theme of the father potentially destroying the thing he cared about most – the ultimate victim being his daughter – seemed to me a classic theme around which to build a story. It seemed to have a particular kind of horror, going back to the Greeks, to Oedipus and Medea, all the great classics' (cited in Weaver 1991: 88).

The greatest exponent of what might be regarded as 'quality' exploitation was producer and director Roger Corman. His adaptations of the Edgar Allan Poe stories *The Fall of the House of Usher* (1960) and *The Pit and the Pendulum* (1961), featuring Vincent Price, created suspense through protracted scenes without dialogue preceding sudden jolts of unexpected violence or disorder. The 'trash' end of exploitation, from William Castle onwards, ironically proved more influential. Graphic realism came to radicalise the form and oppose the conservative tendencies of romanticism (see Vale and Juno 1986; Newman 1988; Paul 1994; Cartmell 1997; Chibnall 1998).

As Universal International's 'weirdie' films proliferated, and James Carreras continued to establish Hammer's credentials in the global marketplace, AIP, headed by Samuel Z. Arkoff and James H. Nicholson, jumped on the teen-horror bandwagon with *I Was a Teenage Werewolf* (1957) and *I Was a Teenage Frankenstein* (1957). Recognising that theatres needed more than blockbuster 'A' pictures, and using the attractive economy of the double bill, AIP produced films to exploit the burgeoning youth market. Exploitation pictures of this sort often began only with the excessive promise of a title rich in hyperbole, an action packed trailer, an exhaustive marketing campaign, William Castle-like gimmickry and the implication of transgression. Sometimes subject to the opposition of the authorities and advocacy groups, AIP maintained an ethical stance to their film-making by arguing that these films were essentially black comedies, whose themes and issues of teenage alienation were fully understood by their audience. Tony (Michael Landon), the hero of *I Was a Teenage Werewolf*, for example, is hypnotically regressed into the figure of a werewolf; the monster here merely a literalisation of marginalisation within teen peer groups and the generational divide in 1950s America.

Roger Corman, both at AIP and in his own New World Pictures, became an increasingly influential figure. His most significant works in the genre remain his adaptations of the Poe stories, which echoed the lush and sometimes ponderous style of the Hammer films, but achieved their most affecting moments in scenes pregnant with anticipation. *The Fall of the House of Usher, The Pit and the Pendulum, Tales of Terror* (1962), *The Premature Burial* (1962), *The Masque of the Red Death* (1964) and *The Tomb of Legeia* (1965) – all but *The Premature Burial*, featuring Vincent Price – comment on the slow disintegration of the nuclear family through psychological instability and the engagement with perverse pleasures in the pursuit of power. The monster here is madness, and the limits of the human sensibility. Corman's detached style merely exacerbates the intensity and inevitability of personal and social collapse (see Hogan 1986).

However it was Hammer, in their combination of Guignol and exploitation, who advanced the genre. *Curse of Frankenstein* (1957), following on from the sombre invasion narrative of *The Quatermass Xperiment* (1955), was groundbreaking in playing the Baron (Peter Cushing) as a wholly rational, if obsessive professional scientist. As Hardy has noted, 'the Baron and his creature are complementary figures, each embodying what the other lacks ... while the Baron seeks to create a perfected version of himself, what his creatures reflect back at him are his own moral flaws and emotional atrophy' (1985: 107). In *Revenge of Frankenstein* (1958) the Baron effectively becomes his own creation when he insists that his brain is transplanted into his creature, who looks exactly like him. This, ironically, worked *within* the British realist tradition; so much so that Peter Cushing consulted his local doctor concerning accuracy in the use of surgical instruments and medical procedures for operations. The objective aesthetic in these films, visible in the work of Terence Fisher (see Pirie 1973; Ringel 1975), Hammer's most obviously 'auteurist' director, often renders them inhibited and literal, despite their occasional visual excesses. Fisher has argued, 'I know that it's popular and fashionable to say that the unseen is the most scaring. I don't believe this! I believe the seen to be the most scaring thing I can think of and the first movement of the Frankenstein monster coming to life was one of them – and that was just a twitch of the hand' (cited in Frank 1981: 67).

This calls into question not merely the notion of 'observing' something, but the nature of involvement for the audience provoked by observing. Fisher's almost documentarist eye serves to objectify horror rather than enhance its subjective suggestion. Ultimately, this supports the conservative agenda through which patriarchal authority fights to ward off the implicit evil of feminine seduction or villainous amorality. The body becomes the site of ideological and ethical conflict, but only in relation to identity rather than through its viscerae. As Chibnall (1998) argues, although the puritan patriarchs take sadistic pleasure in executing Hammer's Byronic, sexually active but highly domesticated Dracula (Christopher Lee), and challenging the winsome charms of voluptuous vampires, this became increasingly unpersuasive in the sexually liberated climate of the 1960s and early 1970s. Although *The Vampire Lovers* (1970), *Lust for a Vampire* (1970) and *Twins of Evil* (1971) (based on Sheridan LeFanu's *Carmilla*) were partially challenging in their soft-core use of the lesbian vampire, the 'camp' aspects of Hammer horror were being more readily foregrounded, and as Ingrid Pitt, Hammer's leading vamp has noted, 'there were always enough volunteers to retrieve my fangs when they kept falling in Kate O'Mara's cleavage'. Ultimately, and perhaps with hindsight, it is clear that the Hammer horrors were only relatively innovative in the genre, but challenging in relation to British Cinema as a whole.

Christopher Lee's portrayal of Dracula as 'romantic, heroic, fascinating, highly dangerous, savage, but tormented, agonised, sad' is indicative in this respect. A surviving relic of feudalism, yet regulated by the increasingly modern context of the nineteenth-century *petit bourgeoisie*, Hammer's Dracula suffers in his quest for authority and erotic pragmatism. His every attempt to re-invent himself is confounded by being stuck within the same social limits (most particularly, class) as well as his condition as the un-dead. There is a ready metaphor here for the ideological struggle Britain engages with in the post-war period; this is most specifically an 'England' that cannot escape its own obligation to the past and remains frustrated in its desire for change (see Durgnat 1970; Pirie 1977). It is perhaps no accident that Britain needed the post-war 'war film' and the *Carry On* cycle. Hammer and the other leading exponents of British horror struggled with these issues, but they succumbed to near-parody, and a mock-exposé of sexual mores.

Anglo-Amalgamated produced what David Pirie has called the 'Sadeian Trilogy' of *Horrors of the Black Museum* (1959), *Circus of Horrors* (1959) and the profoundly influential *Peeping Tom* (1960). The latter was directed by Michael Powell and engaged with the anxieties in British culture regarding sexual repression, patriarchal obsession, voyeuristic pleasure and perverse violence. Critically abhorred on its first release, *Peeping Tom* has since been recognised as one of the genre's problematic master-pieces. Writer Leo Marks, a senior war-time code-breaker, brings his obsession with codes to the film, combining 'the great indecipherable code' of women, 'the greatest code of all ... the unconscious' and the desire to create 'the unbreakable code'. The impossible task in the film is the quest to photograph 'fear' itself. Michael Powell, accused of over-identifying with the central character's relationship to the camera, and in casting his own son as the persecuted boy in the film's 'home movies', essentially explores the 'sexual seepage' of post-war culture and shows compassion for the 'urge to gaze' of Mark Lewis (Karl Boehme), and indeed, his sadistic compulsion to kill in the quasi-rape of his victims with a spike on his camera's tripod. Hutchings (1993) affirms that *Peeping Tom* is a key film, which along with Hitchcock's *Psycho* came to define the new pre-occupations of the genre (see Pirie 1973; Hutchings 1993).

In a number of ways, the ultimately conservative nature of Hammer horror is best understood in the light of the emergent *giallo* films in Italy, or the surreal arbitrariness of much Spanish horror, or the burgeoning horror cinema in Mexico, featuring La Llorona and wrestling, or the low-grade schlock of the American drive-ins, which effectively progressed the genre by mixing trash aesthetics and stylistic bravura. *Giallo* means yellow in Italian. The series of horror films that became the *gialli* gained their

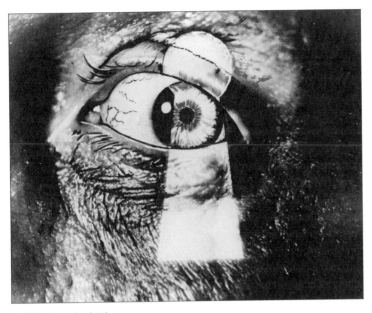

FIGURE 2 *Peeping Tom (1960)*

name from the yellow-covered pulp thrillers that were popular in Italy in the post-war period. Part noir, part brutal melodrama, these texts were often predicated on violent acts and sadistic pleasures. Naturally, this kind of lurid thriller translated readily into horror film, but had a style that was clearly inflected by the whole tradition of European art cinema. The sense of 'cinema' at the heart of some of these texts meant that horror became self-conscious both in regard to the previous traditions of the genre drawn from the American context, but also in the ways that art cinema had drawn upon a whole range of other art forms to enhance its credentials and create a counter cinema to the classical Hollywood style. Consequently, in a film like Ricardo Freda's *Lust of a Vampire* (1956), there is recognition of generic codes and conventions, and an attention to self-conscious styling which recalls and popularises Felliniesque touches and Viscontian composition. Interestingly, it was with this film, the first of its kind since the early 1940s, that the genre took hold (see Hunt 1992; Black 1996).

Fuelled by a lurid romanticism similar to the Hammer films, the Italian horrors soon became more explicit and extreme. Most notable here are Mario Bava's *Black Sunday* (1960), featuring the soon-to-be-iconic actress Barbara Steele as the embodiment of male anxiety about empowered female sexuality, and Freda's notorious *The Terror of Dr Hichcock* (1962), a partial Hitchcock pastiche which opens with scenes of necrophilia and then gets progressively worse. 'The candle of his lust burns brightest in the grave' insists the publicity for the film, not surprisingly heightening its exploitative credentials, but undermining the surreal, poetic, and challenging address of the film itself. It is the combination of abstract design principles – blocks of colour, impactive effects (mist and fog predominant), unusual framing – and bravura narrative events, largely mixing the sordid with gothic 'shock' tactics, that properly distinguishes these films, and once more calls attention to the re-positioning and re-definition of art cinema motifs. Ronato Poselli's *The Vampire and the Ballerina* (1959), for example, explores how people are manipulated by ideas, using the iconography of the occult, and it is clear that the horror text is being used as a psychological space allied to a graphic style rich in allusion, and sometimes arbitrary symbolism as a signifier of its aesthetic difference. This grounding in more indigenous and pan-European inflections of cinema was to distinguish its key directors.

These qualities inform the later work of Dario Argento, who George Romero, director of *Night of the Living Dead*, suggests is 'the Gauguin of film-makers; an expressionist who can tell a story purely visually'. Argento is certainly experimental; using subjective point-of-view shots, slow-motion, and dynamically moving cameras to fully aestheticise, and thus complicate, the relationship between the beautiful and the repugnant, the sacred and the profane, and the limits of seeing and feeling. *Suspiria* (1976) and *Inferno* (1980) remain among his best works, even if they are atypical of the more *gialli*-influenced films, showing how psychological insights can mix freely with almost operatic excess (see Jones 1983; Newman 1988). In recent years the work of Michele Soavi and Mariano Baino has continued this tradition (see Kermode 1993). However, perhaps one of the most significant points to note about Italian horror is its intrinsic influence on the emergence of the 'Franchise' film in the US. *Bay of Blood* (1971) bears a striking resemblance to *Friday the 13th*, for example, while *Planet of the Vampires* (1965) has clearly influenced the *Aliens* series.

While the Italian tradition has gained notoriety on the world stage, it is not alone within the European context in providing fresh and complex re-workings of gothic motifs. Spaniard Jesus Franco's quasi-softcore surrealism in *The Awful Dr Orloff* (1962), *Lesbian Vampires* (1970), *The Bare-Breasted Countess* (1975), *Necromonicon* (1967), *Cannibals* (1979), and *Sadomania* (1980) represents a self-aware, low-rent approach to genre staples, and arguably this in itself stretches boundaries both by default and design. In many senses, Franco's work operates as a model of *incoherent cinema**, utterly pre-occupied with the possibilities of the medium rather than the demands of the material or a particular story. Franco's pleasure in the voyeuristic aspects of the medium thus brings together horror, humour, pornography, and art cinema in a form seemingly beyond categorisation as each approach seamlessly blurs into the other. His engagement with cinema has made him one of the most prolific film-makers of all time, and while there is considerable inconsistency in his output, his one-man assault on the censorious aspects of politics, religion, and culture in Spain may be viewed as both the resistance of the radical 'amateur' and the eccentric bravura of a self-styled showman.

The early 1970s were a halcyon period for Spanish horror. Leon Klimovsky's *The Werewolf's Shadow* (1970) proved an international success, and spawned many werewolf movies. Styled on the Universal Lon Chaney series, the werewolf, more often than not played by actor Paul Neschy, symbolised the challenging transition of an apparently ordinary man; his orality and violence acting as a persuasive metaphor of rebellion against oppression and conservatism in Spain, and an overt nod to the pleasures of consumption. The other key 'monster' of this period was Amando de Ossorio's un-dead Knight Templar, who featured in *Tombs of the Blind Dead* (1971).

Similar work emerged from France and Poland, and even in Bollywood and China, each signifying an indigenous take on the orthodoxies of the horror film, underpinned by local preoccupations and the established traditions of each national cinema. The Bollywood context is especially interesting as it foregrounds the work of the seven Ramsay brothers, who inherited their father's film-making franchise and continued his tradition of horror movies. Grounded in religious contexts which play out archetypal, if culturally inflected, conflicts between good and evil, the Ramsays' films speak to local superstitions; the 'night-time' confluence of fear and fornication; the necessarily epic nature of many Bollywood films; and the particular demographic of the horror fan, an unusually specific audience in the Indian context. For the sake of cultural decorum, and sensitivity to particular dogma, the demon is nearly always vanquished, and the gods prevail. What remains clear, however, is that despite the indigenous framing of such movies, Hollywood may still be evidenced: *Purani Haveli* (1989) is essentially an 'old dark house' film, and *Mahakaal* (1994) is a re-run of Wes Craven's *Nightmare on Elm Street*.

La Llorona is an enduring horror phenomenon indigenous to Mexican fantasy cinema. First featured in *The Crying Woman* (1933), and the subject of many inflections in ancient folklore, la Llorona is a woman, brutalised by men, and driven to murder or torture her children. Her subsequent madness leads her to suicide, or sometimes provokes her execution, and she returns to wreak havoc on earth as a crying mother in search of her children. This lachrymose spirit, along with dead monks (see *The Phantom of the Convent* (1934)) and a violin-playing leper (*The Mystery of the Pallid Face* (1934)) is part of the dominant trend of supernatural horror in 1930s Mexico. Fu Manchu thrillers followed in the 1940s, featuring American-cum-Oriental stage magician David Bamberg, anticipating the increasingly symbiotic relationship between what might be termed 'variety' performers and the horror genre. This is at its most explicit when wrestling became an integral part of the genre in the 1960s, with figures like Santo and Blue Demon, doing battle with incongruous villains in films like *Samson vs The Vampire Women* (1961) and *Blue Demon vs The Infernal Brains* (1967). Indeed, Mexican horror may be viewed as a tension between, and a juxtaposition of, fantasy elements and the persistence of the everyday. This means that wrestlers, werewolves and winos can occupy the same space and provide a vivid portrayal of a highly resistant sub-culture. In such a world peasants can triumph, masked wrestlers can maintain some sense of morality and monsters can be seen in the light of 'magic realism'; what Fredric Jameson has described as 'a *metamorphosis** in perception and things perceived', in which the content constructs 'not a realism to be transfigured by the "supplement" of a magical perspective but a reality which is already in and of itself magical or fantastic', constituted from 'the articulated superposition of whole layers of the past within the present' (1992: 128–54).

Mexican horror calls upon historic myths and legends to play them out in often violent spectacle. Seminal works like *Bodysnatcher* (1956), *The Vampire* (1957) and *The Baron of Terror* (1961) all call upon more familiar gothic themes, but only when Mexican horror calls upon its own past – the Aztecs, snake cults, folkloric tattooing rituals, demonic spirits – that its impact on the genre may be fully appreciated (see Wilt 1995). Perhaps the most well known of South American film-makers, Chilean Alejandro Jodorowsky, engages with similar material in his two most famous works, *El Topo* (1970) and *Sante Sangre* (1989). He argues:

I made some echoes from horror films, but I played with them ... There's the Invisible Man, and a zombie scene from Romero, but in *Night of the Living Dead* they were terrible persons coming back from the dead, and these are beautiful women. It is anti-terror. In *The Invisible Man,* he suffered because he wants to be visible. Here he takes off his bandages and suffers because he is *still* visible. He wants to disappear because he doesn't like himself as a criminal. So here am I playing with horror, and at the same time I am making anti-horror.

In this light then, Hammer may be viewed as the last vestige of consensus and constraint before the 'bindings of the bodice' finally snapped. Chills, chuckles and chain saws were to follow in the new age of chaos and collapse.

3   CHAOS AND COLLAPSE 1960-2000

Psycho

The impact of Alfred Hitchcock's *Psycho* cannot be underestimated. As David Hogan has noted, '*Psycho* redefined the horror genre not only in terms of graphicism, but in matters of tone' (1986: 189). Horror films before *Psycho*, whatever their intensity or effect, were essentially narratives that operated within necessary limits that offered closure and security. Further, and most significantly, identification and empathy in such films were determined by the movie-goer. *Psycho* sought to challenge this perspective by directly implicating the viewer in an amoral universe grounded in the psychic imperatives of its protagonists (see Truffaut 1986). As Bronfen suggests, Norman Bates (Anthony Perkins) 'both is and is not mother, both is and is not dead, is neither masculine nor feminine, mother nor son, fetish, corpse, nor living body. Rather it is all these states amalgamated into one phantastic body, into whose presence Hitchcock has drawn us' (1998: 31). This is merely one of numerous readings of *Psycho*, of course, but it does posit the idea of the modern monster as mutable, protean, unspeakable, unknowable, but ironically, and frighteningly, domesticated. Norman Bates is the 'boy next door', the completely familiar.

Based on the true story of Ed Gein, a Wisconsin farmer who murdered and mutilated a number of young women and his mother, sometimes eating their bodies, preserving their flesh, and using body parts for household furnishings and functions, *Psycho* locates shockingly transgressive events in an everyday context, subject to ordinary conditions. Its impressionist brutalities – most notable in the shower murder of Marion Crane (Janet Leigh) – are matched only by its ambivalence as the narrative plunges into previously unimaginable areas of human degradation, which in their actuality seem to re-define all before it as acceptable fantasy. Crucially, though, it is the effectiveness with which Hitchcock first manipulates our sympathy for Marion, when she absconds with $40,000, and then Norman, whom we accept is only covering up for his mother's murderous crimes, that invites the audience to consider its position. Any clear sense of right or wrong has been irradicated, and the world is seen to be an amoral and random place. This world is everyday America, represented as an utterly remote place in which any semblance of moral or ethical security has been destabilised and proved to be illusory. As Stephen Rebello has noted, the film delights in 'skewering America's sacred cows – virginity, cleanliness, privacy, masculinity, sex, mother love, marriage, the reliance on pills, the sanctity of the family ... and the bathroom' (1990: 46).

Such themes had been addressed elsewhere, of course; the psychosexual problems in Corman's Poe adaptations, male anxiety and marital instability in the 'creature features', the unspeakable acts conducted in private in many of the 'mad scientist' narratives. However, a horror film had never previously had the legitimacy of one of cinema's acknowledged masters – Alfred Hitchcock, a distinctly modernist address at its heart, and the previously latent dynamics of psychoanalysis as a prominant part of the story itself (see Jankovich 1996). *Psycho* essentially defines the parameters of the text *and* sub-text of the genre as a whole. It is the moment when the monster, as a metaphor or myth, is conflated with the reality of a modern world in which humankind is increasingly self-conscious and alienated from its pre-determined social structures. *Psycho* works as an act of permission for film-makers in the genre to further expose the illusory securities and limited rationales of contemporary life to reveal the chaos which underpins modern existence and constantly threatens to ensure its collapse.

Robert Bloch's narrative conceit of murdering the heroine unusually early in the narrative, Joseph Stefano's taboo-challenging screenplay, Saul Bass's lateral yet impressionistic design and Bernard Herrmann's score all contribute to making *Psycho* a different model of the horror film, but inevitably it is Hitchcock's stylistic bravura which make the film a determinedly modernist engagement with the genre. This can be seen in sequences such as Marion's journey to the Bates Motel (echoing a similar journey to Mandaley in his earlier gothic, *Rebecca* (1940)), the shower-bath murder, the murder of detective Arboghast and the discovery of 'mother'. The film challenged permitted orthodoxies in relation to sex, sexuality, violence and social identity, and it did so with an aesthetic sensibility which justified itself as 'art', and insisted upon the necessity of addressing the material seriously. However, it is ultimately Hitchcock's black humour – Bates' affiliation to birds, the suspense as the car containing Marion's dead body initially fails to sink in the swamp, the insistent voice of 'mother' – which exposes the irony of modernity, a tone and an approach to be much imitated.

Arguably, *Psycho* inspires the two dominant paradigms of the horror film in the late twentieth century. Firstly, in identifying, implicitly summating and definitively expressing the core meanings of the horror genre: psycho-sexual and psychosomatic angst, non-socialised violent imperatives, the instability and inappropriate nature of established socio-cultural structures and the oppressive omnipresence of 'death', *Psycho* 'ends' the horror movie, and ushers in the *postmodern* era in the genre. As Fred Botting confirms, after *Psycho* these key themes, already subject to ambiguity and contradiction in many texts, become increasingly 'unstable, unfixed and ungrounded in any reality, truth or identity other than those that the narratives provide, and there emerges a threat of sublime excess, of a new darkness of multiple and labyrinthine narratives, in which human myths again dissolve, confronted by an uncanny force beyond its control' (1996: 171). The second model may be viewed as *ambivalent realism*, and is predicated on locating horror in a realist context but playing out an essentially amoral agenda or determining a scenario where moral or ethical certainty is unattainable. Ultimately, both models promote excess in the genre, and refuse the consensus and constraint of much in the pre-*Psycho* years.

Alfred Hitchcock, one of cinema's great directors, was not synonymous with the horror genre before his work on *Psycho*. His credentials as the master of suspense were established in thrillers like *Blackmail* (1929), *Sabotage* (1936), *Suspicion* (1941), *Shadow of a Doubt* (1943), *Strangers on a Train* (1951), *Rear Window* (1954) and *Vertigo* (1958), all of which engage with psychopathic, murderous imperatives as they are played out in an apparently amoral universe. In many ways, the obsessive figure of Scottie Ferguson (James Stewart) in *Vertigo*, in his desperate attempts to re-fashion the dead Madeleine, through his insistent transformation of Judy and the subsequent suggestion of necrophiliac fulfilment anticipates the psycho-sexual perversion of Norman Bates. The Oedipal trajectory is also writ large in *The Birds* (1963), where the 'revenge of nature' is aroused by a mother's resistance to her son's relationship. However, the brutal attacks of the birds signify more in the sense that they defy humanity's ability to defend itself. This quiet, almost ambivalent apocalypse remains deeply threatening in its horror. One member of the focus group interviewed for this project recalls, 'It was the day after *The Birds* had been shown on television and I was walking through Holland Park in central London. I saw a group of children, who had just visited the Commonwealth Institute, dive to the floor as a flock of pigeons rose into the air ...'

Drive-in dread

In 1963 Hershall Gordon Lewis made an exploitation picture called *Blood Feast*, and with it invented what Vale and Juno (1986) have called the sub-genre of 'intensive gore' films. A brain is removed from a skull, legs are amputated and a tongue is pulled from a young girl's head in gory detail, yet with no small degree of humour. Implausible, exaggerated, poorly executed and politically incorrect, it satiated an appetite in the popular audience for ever more bloody excesses. In the same year, the pseudo-anthropological documentary *Mondo Cane* (1963) showed tribal activities with unusual rituals of animal abuse, human sacrifice and primitive customs, spawning a further sub-genre of *mondo* movies, all exploiting supposedly authentic yet horrifically titillating rites in a number of foreign or marginalised contexts. Kim Newman (1988) has suggested that these films were a key influence on the cannibal films made in Italy during the 1970s and the theme of cannibalism, in general, during the period. Cannibal films in the Italian context constitute an indigenous sub-genre, effectively beginning with *Cannibal* (1976) and *Cannibal Holocaust* (1979), directed by Ruggero Deodato, which mounts a critique of exploitation film-making in the Third World and ends with the final irony of cannibals, driven to sensationalist excess by the film-makers, eating their provocateurs. However, it is *Cannibal Ferox* (1980), directed by Umberto Lenzi, which remains notorious for its depiction of 'convincing scenes in which a cannibal hacks off a penis and eats it, a woman is hung from meathooks in her breasts, an eye is fished out with a knife, [and] a villain's skull is sliced like a breakfast egg so his brains can be scooped out and eaten.' (Newman 1988: 193).

The post-*Psycho* years, it seems, opened the floodgates for horror intrinsically related to bodily torture and mutilation. Arguably, and certainly in the case of Italian film-maker, Lucio Fulci, in a film like *The Beyond* (1981), violence could be translated into an exploration of carnivalesque grotesquery and the prioritisation of sensation and effect over the motivations of plot. However, in many senses, Italian horror had always been characterised by this approach.

The most notable aesthetic imitations in the *Psycho* model were the stalker movies; *Halloween*, directed by John Carpenter, *Friday the 13th*, directed by Sean Cunningham, and *Graduation Day* (1981), directed by Herb Freed. Vera Dika has suggested that these films, and numerous others like them, share a formula which is often predicated on simultaneity of the commemoration of a previous murder or violation in the past and a historically determined social ritual (halloween, prom night and so on), and ultimately deal with 'the overvaluation of family ties, the viewing of the primal scene (or its variant in acts of illicit sexuality or violently unlawful actions) and the horrible consequences of such perversions' (1990: 17). The key defining element in these films, however, is the unseen presence of the 'stalker' and the ensuing suspense which is caused by not knowing where the monster is, or when the murderer will strike. The free-flowing movement of the camera and the sustained use of point-of-view shots are often signifiers of the murderer's approach, arguably implicating the audience in the violence that follows. More plausibly, the audience is merely situated in the best place to observe the extreme effects of violence, or often, in more orthodox constructions of the *mise-en-scène*, made to observe the unseen monster in the back of the frame, ready to pounce. The pantomime-like chants of 'he's behind you' in cinemas during such scenes do much to make these moments as comic as they are potentially horrifying, especially as the audience will almost certainly be distracted again before the monster finally leaps and surprises everyone. Dika has argued that 'the audience of the stalker film responds as a group, regardless of the class or the social background of that audience' (1990: 17).

The body counts in these films are high, and the acts of violence of a primitive nature, usually enacted with a knife, an axe, or a similar sharp instrument. This supports readings of the films as sadistic rape-oriented narratives or misogynist texts (see Clover 1992). Arguably, here the monster may also be read as a moral force, excessively punishing the young for immoral and amoral acts. Equally, the monster may be viewed as a symbolic embodiment of evil incarnate – a historically-determined 'loose cannon', psychopathically reaping as a consequence of some past misdeed and ultimately undefeatable. The focus groups who spoke of these films noted their enjoyment of the chase aspects of these narratives and the oscillation between fearing for the victim, fearing the presence and eventual actions of the monster itself, and fearing their own (and others') responses to the outcomes of events, even if these proved to be laughter rather than screams. Crucially, however, all spoke of knowing that they were instrumental in the artifice of such movies because they recognised the conventions. These postmodern texts show what Clover describes as 'the explicitness of these murders and the superreal rendition of their special effects make-up ... counterposed to the reduced reality in the presentation of the film's victims. The latter's two-dimensional quality has made possible this explicit gore, allowing us to see the wound without the appropriate levels of fear or regret' (1992: 71). The self-consciousness of these films enables them to pastiche the genre while extending the limits of what it may depict and what it may reflect culturally. As Crane has suggested, this largely amounts to the fact that 'all collective action will fail; knowledge and experience have no value when one is engaged with the horrible; and the destruction of the menace (should it occur) carries no guarantee that the future will be safe' (1994: 10).

'They're coming to get you, Barbara'

George Romero's low-budget black and white film *Night of the Living Dead* (1968) provides a further turning point in contemporary horror. Its subversiveness echoes the radical politics of the period, its approach both parodies and advances generic expectations and its message reinforces the dystopic tendencies of the post-*Psycho* period. The 'dead' return as zombies, possibly revived by radiation, killing and cannibalising all those before them. Uncertainty prevails, and any notion of 'society' collapses in the light of this silent but relentless rebellion. The mass of zombies, 'the silent majority', operate as an unstoppable force which echoed the images of riot in Paris and the implicit demise of old institutions. Romero suggests that 'It came out of the anger of the times. No one was gleeful at the way that the world was going, so these political themes were addressed in the film. The zombies could be the dead in Vietnam; the consequence of our mistakes in the past, you name it ...'.

Romero's generic inflections are similarly pertinent. Brother and sister Johnny (Russell Streiner) and Barbara (Judith O'Dea) visit their father's grave to lay a wreath. Johnny teases Barbara as she is approached by what appears to be a tramp in the graveyard. 'They're coming to get you, Barb,' he says with Karloff-like glee. However, the figure is a monster, a zombie who kills Johnny and renders Barbara catatonic with shock. Barbara escapes and finds protection with the film's black hero Ben

FIGURE 3 *Night of the Living Dead (1968)*

(Duane Jones), who in turn finds refuge with other survivors, including bigot Harry Cooper (Karl Hardman). Unfortunately, and challengingly, it is Ben who proves to be wrong when he suggests remaining potentially mobile on the ground floor while Harry suggests barricading themselves in the cellar. The zombies eventually enter. Harry's daughter Karen (Kyra Schon) ultimately eats her mother, Johnny returns and eats his sister, and finally, when Ben leaves the house to greet a group of potential saviours, he is shot, suspected of being a zombie.

The film, both witty and subversive, was influenced by EC Comics, and again, by Hitchcock, this time in relation to *The Birds*. Pessimistic, and resisting any degree of sentiment, *Night of the Living Dead* suggests that all of the consensual bonding that was possible in previous models of 'community-under-threat' has now dissipated into petty feuding and almost wilful misunderstanding predicated on each person's belief in their own intrinsic 'rightness'. As Romero suggests, 'the most frightening thing is that nobody communicates. Everybody is isolated and alone with their own version of the world. They're all kinda insane. The trouble is that they can see that the afterlife is no better. Even if you're good there are no guarantees'. It is in this relativism that the film reveals its truly dystopic nature. The monster here is the embodiment of the revelation that the machinations of the world are unstoppable and inevitably destructive and meaningless. Romero's sequels *Dawn of the Dead* (1978) and *Day of the Dead* (1985) merely extend these premises to expose the collapse of consumer capitalism, the inevitable lack of fulfilment in current models of existence and the deep anger that still fuels the limited desire to find alternatives and to somehow create a new society. Romero is ultimately a dark satirist exposing the profound fragmentation in social structures and the complete vulnerability inherent in any one individual's life expectancy.

Repulsion to Rosemary

Roman Polanski's horror films of the 1960s – *Repulsion* (1965), *Dance of the Vampires* (1967) and *Rosemary's Baby* (1968) – effectively summate the progress of the genre from what Andrew Tudor (1989) has called 'secure' horror. In these films the forces of rationality are mobilised to restore order, to the state of 'paranoid' horror, in which all notions of an established and transparent status quo are suspended or challenged.

Arguably, Polanski also plays out tensions between ambivalent realism and the postmodern form of horror text by not merely engaging with personal and social determinacy, especially in the lives of women, but re-configuring the spectacle of the horror film by further pastiching known styles — most particularly, Hammer's gothic romanticism and the post-*Psycho* thriller's urban ambience. Virginia Wright Wexman suggests that Polanski's 'horror films do not simply illustrate cultural processes that victimise and warp the powerless; they ask us to re-capitulate our own participation in such processes, and they expose the structures of domination that popular conventions naturalise. The subject of Polanski's horror films is not others but otherness itself' (1985: 48). In depicting 'otherness' in the hallucinations and murderous psychoses of Carol Ledoux (Catherine Deneuve) in *Repulsion*, the dance of aristocratic corpses chillingly absent in the 'social' mirror in *Dance of the Vampires*, and the neurotic pregnancy of Rosemary Woodhouse (Mia Farrow) in *Rosemary's Baby*, Polanski wittily demonstrates the deep unreliability of the body and the mind, and how their increasing dissociation merely exposes how each has been corrupted, re-determined or rendered inappropriate in the changing social climate.

Rosemary's Baby remains particularly effective in drawing together archetypal, religiously-oriented myths (fear of rape by the Devil, the primitive 'magic' of witches, satanist practices) with modern pathologies about domestic economy, health and the body. By prioritising the fears of women Polanski further radicalises the genre. Crucially, *Rosemary's Baby* playfully engages with empathy and identification in the sense that we are offered Rosemary's perspective and necessarily must believe that her life is being determined by satanist conspiracy, otherwise our own sanity, sense of perspective, and rational order are also questioned and irradicated. By addressing religion, the impact of children, and in playing out conspiracy, *Rosemary's Baby* thus wrestles with powerful social anxieties and anticipates the ways in which the horror film would configure the body as the key site of ideological and creative struggle.

Religion has been a determining aspect of the horror film throughout its history, but as writer and director Paul Schrader has noted, '*The*

Exorcist was particularly effective because it managed, in a commercial story-telling mode, to get God and the Devil in the same room discussing issues of good and evil over the body of a thirteen year old girl'. Consequently, the sense of struggle in the film is especially pertinent because the victim is a child, and the outcome of the battle is crucial to the sense of how the future will be newly configured. Arguably, the film is merely a parental fantasy in which a deeply troubled adolescent is coerced through a period of rebellion into maturity, reinforcing patriarchal authority along the way. On another level, however, the metaphoric struggle between the maintenance of the sacred, humanistic, and philosophically enshrined, in the face of profanity, brutalism and decay was self-evidently persuasive in the minds of the audience. The film soon transcended its archetypal narrative and gained notoriety for its apparent social effects. Audiences responded to the film in a variety of ways – vomiting, urinating, fainting, miscarrying – and were supposedly prompted into behaviour ranging from acts of petty crime through to a full-time commitment to the occult. One mother described her experience on a BBC Radio phone-in: 'My daughter woke me up. She was screaming in her sleep. This went on for three weeks. For an eighteen year old girl to come to her mother's bed and ask to be comforted. She hadn't done that since she was three years old. She is still disturbed.'

Images of a young girl masturbating with a crucifix, vomiting over a priest, shouting obscenities and possessing unusual physical dexterities prevented the BBFC from granting a video release until 1999. As the focus groups watching the film now report, however, the film's excesses seem more preposterous than profound, but its folkloric status and enduring sense of physical and material struggle are still engaging. *The Exorcist* remains important in that it drew the horror genre into mainstream commercial cinema and found a major audience which were not merely horror fans. Further big-budget horror films followed which also concentrated on similar themes, most notably *The Omen* (1976) and *The Sentinel* (1977). *Jaws* (1975) also became a phenomenal box-office success and clearly demonstrates the generic characteristics of the horror film.

The horror film in the post-*Psycho* era has also seen the systematic collapse of assurance in, and promotion of, the family and conservative family values. Children, once the epitome of innocence and ideological neutrality, become configured as the monster, partly to illustrate the proliferation of 'evil' as a natural phenomenon, and to exemplify the inevitability of 'evil' in the nurturing process, the latter effectively showing children as the product of adult misconduct. Mark Jancovich has noted that 'in a culture where women are primarily responsible for child-rearing, the child can come to be seen as a demanding vampire-like figure, who dominates the mother and threatens to destroy her' (1992: 111). Stephen King suggests that 'kids are different. They can be totally uncivilised, and not very nice. But they have special qualities. They are constantly in a state of shock about new stuff, and just don't know how to be "civilised" about it, so they do all this different stuff instead, good and bad'.

The murderous, remorseless child of *The Bad Seed* (1956) was one of the earliest examples in which the otherness of children is used to explore transgression and threat. *Rosemary's Baby* and *The Exorcist* propelled the 'devil child' into the mainstream, but it was Larry Cohen's *It's Alive!* (1973), with its unplanned and unwanted baby, bent on revenge, that says much about the complex symbiotic relationship between parent and child and its unpredictable effects. Cohen remarks:

It's Alive! tries to tell about parents' feelings for a child that's different. In today's world it could be anything wrong with the kid – psychologically or physiologically – and yet parents have to come to terms with their feelings for the child. At the time I made the picture, people were afraid of their children because their kids were wearing their hair long, smoking grass, and fucking ... and there was a general fear of the younger generation by the older generation.

(cited in Vale and Juno 1986: 118)

Cohen's later works *It Lives Again* (1978) and *It's Alive III: Island of the Alive* (1987) deal with the issue of abortion, the United States judiciary, anxiety about AIDS and the impact of the media and marketing. The popularity of these films among female audiences indicates that the idea of pregnancy as what Linda Ruth Williams (1989) has called 'graphic possession' has some currency, and that monster babies are merely an exaggerated depiction of the more troubling aspects of child develop-ment. Films like *Parents* (1989), about quiet, God-fearing, suburban cannibals, *The Stepfather* (1986), concerning a serial monogamist murdering straying step-families and *Society* (1990), literally showing the fleshly symbiosis of the class system, all wittily engage with the collapse of the moral order in the family unit, citing it as not merely the repository of horrific acts but the cause of them (see Stanbrook 1990).

If this were not enough, 'conspiracy' culture has been a key element of the sci-fi/horror/thriller films of the era since the Kennedy assassination. Although the theme has best manifested itself in political films like *The Conversation* (1974), *The Parallax View* (1974), *All the President's Men* (1976) and *Marathon Man* (1976), a general undercurrent in contemporary horror is the suppression and revelation of knowledge and information which will have a direct effect on the known orthodoxies of lived experience. Writer and director Wes Craven says of *Nightmare on Elm Street*, 'I like to bring larger issues to horror films; I'm not interested in making films that are just a rollercoaster ride. I want to address fears – trivial fears, like falling off a building; cliffhangers, if you like – but also major fears too, like when one generation tells lies to the next and causes real harm'. This sense of secrecy and betrayal underpins many of the 'urban myths' which re-constitute the monster as something that will inevitably re-visit its site of origination or destruction. Fundamentally, this monster is usually grounded in some real event, and its return works as a historical refusal; sins will be re-visited and cannot be repressed or denied. In many senses, this is a key theme of the gothic, and gains greater credibility from its complex reconfiguration in the information era, where it would seem that all private things may soon be knowable, available aspects of the public domain. In the postmodern text, shock emerges not from the revelation of a key piece of information which exposes the corruption at the heart of known and trusted figures and social structures, but from the relentless proliferation of open secrets which serve to mask any one dominant paradigm of significance, stability and security. Everything appears to be a lie, and the truth seemingly unknowable.

Who will survive and what will be left of them?

The Texas Chainsaw Massacre (1974), directed by Tobe Hooper, is a key example of the rural gothic, which like *Night of the Living Dead* calls upon the brutalities of a mythic past and distorts the imperatives and philosophy of frontier life. Self-determination, survivalism, familial loyalty and the progress in settlement become the depraved and corrupted conventions of a backwoods family slaughterhouse, where the chainsaw-wielding 'Leatherface' treats all human life as 'meat'. *The Texas Chainsaw Massacre*, from its slaughterhouse *mise-en-scéne* of bones and flesh configured into a surreal living space, through its sudden sledgehammer attacks, to its extended persecution of Sally (Marilyn Burns), shows only contempt for the body, and with it the tangible credentials of humanity. This theme preoccupies much contemporary horror.

Wes Craven's *Last House on the Left* (1972), which depicts parental revenge on their daughter's rapist murderers, contrives that all are driven by the same desire, whatever their motivation, and however justifiable, to eradicate all vestiges of what it is to know or be human in a 'civilised' way. This kind of 'body-in-pieces' horror seemingly has little social merit, whatever its 'art'. *I Spit on Your Grave* (1978), a 'rape-revenge' movie with protracted scenes of physical violence, and *The Driller Killer* (1979), featuring the murders of homeless itinerants with a drill, again effectively de-humanise. The underlying problem here is one which suggests that the essence of humanity *is* to be violent, anti-social and auto-satisfied, and that socialising structures merely attempt to prevent, hide, or police these tendencies. Through this reading radical imperatives emerge in the films. Wes Craven has argued, for example, that *Last House on the Left* seeks 'to show what violence is *actually* like, and how it really affects us. It's a comment on how the violence in Vietnam became television "junk", and

FIGURE 4 *The Texas Chainsaw Massacre (1974)*

didn't affect anybody anymore. I tried not to make the violence romantic or attractive, but "real", so people would be affected, and speak out against it.'

In a contemporary era in which the unspeakable, unimaginable, and unthinkable have all been dramatised in both ambivalent realist and postmodern texts, these aims are laudable. Yet they essentially dispose of the persuasiveness of metaphor and cast the monster as the audience, who are asked to recognise themselves, only to endorse or resist the representations they see. It is perhaps little wonder that the film-makers themselves, as well as academics, cultural critics and legislators have been necessarily drawn into the debate. Craven attests 'that *someone* has to take responsibility for preserving values, so it is important to shock people into a full recognition that ethics, morality, everyday "getting-along" ... are under tremendous threat, and it's likely that things won't hold up'.

'A virus is trying to live its own life'

Body horror* in the films of David Cronenberg has a different perspective, but is no less apocalyptic. His preoccupation with disease, decay, and malfunction recognises that these elements inform everyday human self-consciousness. Unusually, Cronenberg sees these issues in a more objective light. For example he refuses to emphasise the damaging aspects of a virus on human life, concentrating instead on the imperatives of the virus itself: 'A virus is trying to live its own life; the fact that its destroying you by doing it is not its fault'. In *Shivers* (1975), Cronenberg explores the idea of the body being infected by a sexually-transmitted parasite which ensures its further transmission by acting as an aphrodisiac, and works to de-stabilise the rationality which underpins social structures. Reduced to libidinous and violent chaos, the world is on the edge of imminent collapse. Cronenberg argues, 'it's about repression and restriction; it tries to remove responsibility from the equation, and look at how certain more instinctive drives might work'. Unlike the anxiety experienced by the pregnant Rosemary, Cronenberg's parasitic bug insists upon a perverse eroticism. 'It's a very sexual thing; you want to know what's inside you; you want to know what's driving you to do certain things'. In essence, the film works as a critique of middle-class ethics and socially-determined sexual attitudes, mining the grotesque excesses of the idea. *Rabid* (1976) features a female vampire with a phallic under-arm spike, which again provokes anti-social action in those who are 'vampirised'. In both cases, the crises are provoked by failures in medical science, positing questions of a more 'liberated' culture, but one which unfortunately sees women primarily as provocateurs of social dis-ease. Ironically, Cronenberg's model of ambivalent realism may be viewed as proto-feminist in this respect, if the radical (if unresolved) outcomes are read as the collapse of patriarchy and the usurpation of the phallic.

Cronenberg plays out psychosomatic disorder in the physiological manifestation of psychological states in *The Brood* (1979), telekinetic powers and the political 'ownership' of the body in *Scanners* (1980), hallucinations of physical mutation and reconfiguration in *Videodrome* (1982), transformation and the hybridisation of human flesh, machine, and insect anatomy in *The Fly* (1986), mental breakdown, gynaecological anxiety, and self-determined re-construction in *Dead Ringers* (1988), narcotic consumption and metamorphosis in *Naked Lunch* (1991) and the eroticisation and physical imperatives of damaged bodies in *Crash* (1996). Fundamentally, Cronenberg has articulated the centrality of the body in contemporary horror. He suggests that 'the body is our "material"; flesh and blood ... *is* human life, so I deal with as many concerns about its preservation and continuity as possible. This might mean mutation, evolution, treating everything differently, who knows ...'. In another interview, Cronenberg stresses that the car in *Crash* is merely an extension of his previous technological interests, and another aspect of contemporary civilisation that, if re-determined, would again see social collapse:

If suddenly we said 'There can't be any more cars, we're stopping today', it would be the end of the world: economies diving, people not knowing what to do with themselves. Our attachment to it, as discussed in the movie, is very primitive indeed. It has become the quintessential human appendage. I think it won't go away easily. It's got a lot of shape-shifting to do before it disappears.

(cited in Rodley 1996: 11)

Cronenberg's sense of social disintegration is never far from the relationship between physical needs, human progress and utilitarian contexts created for industrial and economic development.

Barker's bodies

Clive Barker, novelist, artist, writer and director, has already achieved considerable success in two major aspects of the horror genre. Firstly, he has resurrected the notion of British horror which has been mainly understood as a phenomenon of the Hammer Studios. This has thus neglected the work of Anglo-Amalgamated, Amicus and Tigo, the under-rated promise of directors Michael Reeves in *Witchfinder General* (1968) and Peter Sykes in *Demons of the Mind* (1971), and especially, the exploitation pictures of Peter Walker, most notably *Frightmare* (1974). Barker, with his self-conscious re-working and reconfiguration of the British horror tradition, has simultaneously progressed the tradition but also called attention to its neglected backwaters.

Secondly, Barker has added a significant myth to the canon of horror monsters, inventing Pinhead (Doug Bradley) and the cenobites in the *Hellraiser* series; *Hellraiser*, *Hellraiser II: Hellbound* (1988), *Hellraiser III: Hell on Earth* (1992) and *Hellraiser IV: Bloodline* (1996). Horror novelist Ramsay Campbell notes that 'what immediately struck me about *Hellraiser* was the extreme honesty about sado-masochism', and it is in this theme that Barker not merely emphasises the protean nature of the body and identity, but readily draws together issues of eroticism and brutality. Barker's sense of the mutability of the flesh, and the combinative sense of organs and tissue, is played out through characters with ambivalent sexual orientations and the problematics of bodily need. Barker's bodies are concerned with perspectives outside social orthodoxy,

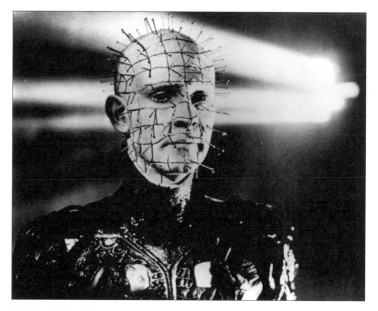

FIGURE 5 *Hellraiser (1987)*

and 'horror' comes out of the fear of a perverse yet partially-desired experience of a marginalised or unknown otherness.

Taking up the work of George Bataille, Joel Black (1991: 121) suggests:

Killing and coitus are pre-eminently *private* acts, intensely personal experiences ... because they impart a wordless kind of knowledge mediated by the body. The carnal knowledge shared by lovers, or by murderer and his victim or witness, does not involve the communication or discursive meaning between two discrete individuals, but a communion at the instant of death between bodies that are no longer distinct from each other.

Barker's work seeks to explore and illustrate the intensity of this 'communion' and the private discourses that underpin it. He significantly differs from Cronenberg in not merely seeing the body in its own self-determined flux, but in addressing issues of control, and the aesthetic of excessive acts upon the body, which may range from self-mutilation to unknowable assault. Sexuality is intrinsically entwined with the pleasures and pains of violent imposition. Barker's work becomes especially important in that he effectively contemporises the sexuality of the horror film through this aesthetic, which, rather than seeking to define pain as the consequence of punishment or attack, embraces it as a model which makes the implied discourse of the gothic – the attraction of the perverse and the transgressive – both a literal and symbolic set of events. Interestingly, this is also given an intrinsically English veneer of aristocratic repression and a tendency to the witty repost – a definition of the villain especially appealing to American audiences, who likewise engaged with Anthony Hopkins as Hannibal Lector in Demme's *Silence of the Lambs*. Like many of the key artistic achievements in recent horror texts, however, the work has been significantly diminished by the rise of 'the sequel' (see Beeler 1994).

The McDonaldisation of horror

Wes Craven made the following observation:

> They wanted Freddy Krueger to be as much amusing as he was scary, and a little more accessible. This is a word they use in Hollywood to mean a little less threatening, a little more commercial. I think their concept of a scary picture was one that wouldn't disturb you but one that would make you jump, and make your date hold you a little closer. It was like making cheeseburgers. You get a formula for something that satisfies the appetite, and then you make it over and over again and make a business out of it.

This is echoed by Stephen King:

> I must say that kids are much more familiar with Ronald McDonald than they are with Jesus or the church. They don't like the Jimmy

Swaggart version of things. Horror fiction gives them something else. Maybe that's why kids read my stuff. It really is the literary equivalent of a Big Mac and fries.

George Ritzer's 'McDonaldisation' thesis (1998) addresses the processes of organisation that underpin consumer society, looking at the social models that lead to highly specified and efficient bureaucratic, industrial, and commercial outcomes. During the 1980s, the horror genre became part of this process, particularly in the franchised series of *Nightmare on Elm Street* and *Friday the 13th* movies, and the proliferation of adaptations of the novels of Stephen King. Ritzer suggests that while 'McDonalds seems to be anything but an American menace ... just beneath the surface is a cold skeletal framework needed for construction of the iron cage of rationalisation' (1998: 79). Ironically, the genre that best epitomised the address of the irrational was being rationalised for a known and committed demographic of horror fans. A clear formula was in place; an ambivalent realist construct in which the monster acts upon a socially familiar context, largely characterised by children and young adults, which operates as a limited, economically secure, but morally indifferent universe. Calculated to deliberately appeal to the very people they were portraying, adaptations of King's work remain intrinsically conservative.

Clive Barker describes Stephen King's work, for example, as informed by 'a Norman Rockwell accessibility. He surrounds his characters with brand names. He seals the moment as a time capsule of consumerism. He then introduces "the darkness", which is usually quite a conventional object or thing, but it is just as *real* as the breakfast that was being eaten before someone gets killed'. Ironically, one of the key themes of King's fiction – the betrayal of humankind by everyday technologies – is at large in the rationalisation of his work for the cinema. Adaptations have been rarely more than efficient: when effective they are essentially the particular vision of their maker, most notably, Stanley Kubrick's strangely distantive sense of the supernatural in *The Shining* (1980) (see Mayersberg 1980; Titterington 1981) and Rob Reiner's mock-excess in *Misery* (1990).

Brian De Palma's *Carrie* (1976) remains the best of the King horror films. Its playful dissection of high school hierarchies works well within the primitive archetypes of 'good' and 'bad' as they are experienced by those who live through them, and as they are expected in the horror text. Carrie (Sissy Spacek) gains the power of telekinesis with the onset of menstruation, and uses her abilities to exact revenge on those who persecute and oppress her; most obviously, her fundamentalist mother and her peers. She is mocked for her ignorance, innocence and burgeoning desire, and destroys both her home and high school as an expression of avenging individuality against a corrupt domestic system. King's skill is in creating a narrative which is both an appealing apocalyptic fantasy and also a ready example of the horror in established and inappropriate power relations and the (arguably redemptive) chaos that would ensue with their collapse.

De Palma has a well-established canon of work within the horror/ thriller genre. Often criticised for his direct pastiche of Alfred Hitchcock's narratives and techniques, he is, however, a film-maker of distinction who enjoys engaging with irony in his suspense sequences, deliberately playing upon the ambivalence of horror and humour. His work in the field includes *Carrie, Sisters* (1973), *The Phantom of the Paradise* (1974), *The Fury* (1978) and *Dressed to Kill* (1980). Joel Black believes that De Palma's work is especially and consistently distinctive in depicting murder 'neither from the detective's, nor the victim's, nor from the killer's point-of-view, but from the perspective of a fourth party – the bystander, who is at once vulnerable and immune to the murderer whose devastation he or she witnesses' (1991: 66). This essentially 'aestheticises' horror violence and problematises the position of the viewing audience.

Aside from the King adaptations, two series of films best epitomise the 'McDonaldisation' process. *Friday the 13th* and *Nightmare on Elm Street*, essentially variations on the stalk 'n' slash movie, spawned a series of sequels featuring their increasingly empathetic central characters; Jason, an automaton mass murderer without clear identity, and Freddy Krueger, the torched child-molester, with an on-going line in the crass *bon mot* and a finger-knife glove. The *Friday the 13th* series ran throughout the 1980s, and the titles are as follows: *Friday the 13th* (1980), *Friday the 13th Part 2* (1981), *Friday the 13th Part 3* (1982), *Friday the 13th: The Final Chapter* (1984), *Friday the 13th Part V: A New Beginning* (1985), *Friday the 13th Part VI: Jason Lives* (1986), *Friday the 13th Part VII: The New Blood* (1988), *Friday the 13th Part VIII: Jason Takes Manhattan* (1989), and *Jason Goes to Hell: The Final Friday* (1993).

The *Nightmare on Elm Street* series is as follows: *A Nightmare on Elm Street* (1984), *A Nightmare on Elm Street Part 2: Freddy's Revenge* (1985), *A Nightmare on Elm Street Part 3: Dream Warriors* (1987), *A Nightmare on Elm Street Part 4: The Dream Master* (1988), *A Nightmare on Elm Street Part 5: The Dream Child* (1989), *Freddy's Dead: The Final Nightmare* (1990), and *Wes Craven's New Nightmare* (1994).

In the early 1990s, New Line Pictures considered the possibility of bringing the two icons together in a Jason vs Freddie 'final conflict'. Robert Englund, who plays Freddy Krueger, comments 'I did not wish to do this project, and they would have had to make me an offer I couldn't refuse to do so. I just thought it had too much of a sense of those old *Abbott and Costello meets the Wolfman* kind of movies, and I didn't want to do that' (see Robb 1998).

In many senses these films are exercises in the cynicism of market-led phenomena in relation to the expression and depiction of a cynical society in which little matters. Common sense, let alone intelligence, is at a premium, and inertia underpins even the most energised of sensations. The 'monsters' become the *frisson* in valueless worlds informed by boredom, inadequacy and the sense that nothing is surprising anymore. Freddy Krueger occupies the vacuity of dreams and becomes the genuine threat that translates them into real nightmares. The reference to the 'Elm Street' of children's primer books, and its coincidental purchase as one of the tributory roads in Dallas where Kennedy was assassinated, adds additional social grounding, but the films' effectiveness lie in their remaining affiliation with the surreal and its juxtaposition with reality.

Jason merely engages in relentless attack. However, the real cynicism lies in the fact that there is no particular answer or response to the

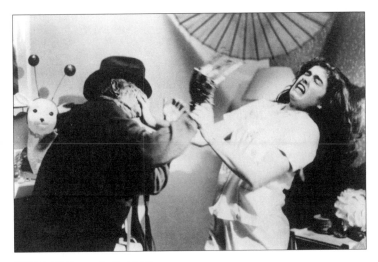

FIGURE 6 *A Nightmare on Elm Street (1984)*

problem of the monster. Jason is anonymous and randomly brutal, Freddy is perverse, vengeful and petty, and yet there are no values, standards, ideas or traditions with which to challenge them. The world is rife with futility. This, perhaps, is why the films ultimately descend into models of black humour. The absurdity informing the conflict between monster and potential victim is effectively meaningless, and, operating purely on the terms, conditions and outcomes of the 'chase', has no terms of reference elsewhere. Its own conventions become the terms of engagement and render the series, despite moments of originality, the epitome of the postmodern text. Indeed, *Wes Craven's New Nightmare, Scream* (1996), and *I Know What You Did Last Summer* (1997) become knowing deconstructions of the sub-genre, and speak only limitedly about the culture that produces them. This is largely because the horror genre has essentially been absorbed into other mainstream genres, or predominantly engages with ambivalent realist models which are re-workings of urban myths, translating the mythic serial killing tendencies of a Freddy or a Jason into ostensibly 'real world' contexts.

Pulling out the buffer of fantasy

This question of the relation between the real and the fantastic is taken up by John McNaughton, who states that 'horror films traditionally incorporate fantasy, which gives you a space to accept that this is not real, and you're protected. We decided to pull out the buffer of fantasy, and make this as real as possible'. McNaughton's *Henry, Portrait of a Serial Killer* (1986), based on the real case of serial killer, Henry Lee Lucas, depicts a number of amoral, seemingly unmotivated, brutal murders. It proved challenging in its removal of known archetypes and its refusal to adopt a clear ethical stance. Former Chairman of the British Board of Film Classification James Ferman notes:

> It does not contain its own moral context within the film. The moral context is brought by the viewer from the outside. It is therefore possible to read *Henry* in any number of ways. It's a morally blank film, and in some ways that's its strength. Forensic experts said it was surprisingly accurate in getting into the psyche of someone who had no feelings for his victim at all.

Crucially, if Jason was a dehumanised, masked model of relentless 'killing-for-fun', the horror is re-introduced when given an ambivalent human face. Henry refuses to engage with the reality of his actions even when gaining fulfilment from them. These actions were deemed problematic when the film was released on video, and the BBFC made cuts in a scene which features the slaughter of a family, in order to show that Henry is actually watching a video recording of his own exploits. McNaughton's intention was to show the murder so that the viewer had a complicit point-of-view in observing the brutalities *before* it was revealed that they were actually watching a video-recording of the events. McNaughton believes these cuts 'lessened the shock and moral impact of the film', while Ferman believes that the Board had to show Henry's point-of-view because it reveals the action of fantasising over video replays of violence rather than being complicit in creating the potential for such things to occur in the viewing home.

It is clear that the power and persuasiveness of *Henry* is in its denial of mythic or 'camp' credentials, and its return to a view of the monster as not merely frightening in its actions, but in its actuality. Further, John McNaughton shows the indifference in contemporary culture by refusing to allow the audience to remove themselves from 'experiencing' Henry's brutalities, or having them explained or finally rationalised. Thus *Henry* potentially re-defines the radical nature of the horror text by exposing and commenting upon the collapse of human values and the instability of the social framework. Cynthia Freeland (1995) argues that *Henry* does, however, privilege the spectacle of violence over narrative, and that this is persuasive because it echoes the conventions of 'reality TV', and the representations of known killers in news bulletins. Further, she argues that the killer is eroticised because he is aligned with the generic codes of 'heroism' in mainstream cinema, and these elements naturalise a climate of gender-encoded violence. Ironically, even though this seems to endorse a conservative perspective, focus groups suggested that they were so used to reassurance through some model of closure in the horror film that this realist ambivalence and sense of social continuum was genuinely troubling. These groups also noted that, without any leavening humour or attractive villainy (in the style of Freddy Krueger) the film also denied them any easy sensations or pleasure from the fulfilment of already-known outcomes (see Sconce 1993).

It is clear from these perspectives that the two crucial elements requiring evaluation in relation to the contemporary horror film are the views of its author and its depiction of a re-determined social context. Steven Spielberg, for example, comments:

Everything I'm afraid of usually comes out somewhere in my movies. Like in *Poltergeist*, I looked at my anxiety about, and apprehension towards, television. Another of my phobias is about bugs and insects, and I have that in *Indiana Jones*. The issue here is the 'realism', because this is not the horror of a "street movie" like *Taxi Driver* or *Henry*. My films are just 'adventures'; things happen when we hide our eyes, but seconds later you remove your hands and enjoy the continuation after the horror.

This mix of the socially acceptable and entertaining with scary effects essentially characterises the 'adult dramas' or 'erotic thrillers' which have become horror movies by another name. These include the key transition film *Fatal Attraction* (1986), and *Silence of the Lambs*, *Sleeping with the Enemy* (1991), *Single White Female* (1992), *Unlawful Entry* (1992), *Basic Instinct* (1992) and *The Hand that Rocks the Cradle* (1992). All feature variations of the sociopath as monster, existing within established parameters of human interaction: romantic bonds, employment relationships, community activities and so on. They imply that any man or woman, dependent upon the lives they lead, the needs they have, and the stress they experience, can become capable of anti-social and brutal acts. Everyone can be a monster if the terms and conditions of their existence are unfulfilling, or if other people prevent them from achieving the promise and potential supposedly available to them in late-capitalist societies. Many of these films explore sociopathic tendencies in women and address the place of women both in society and within the horror text itself, a set of issues best played out in the *Alien* series of films.

At a simplistic level the *Alien* quartet – *Alien* (1979), *Aliens* (1986), *Alien³* (1992), and *Alien Resurrection* (1997) – may be read as a trajectory for Ripley (Sigourney Weaver). She establishes herself as a senior professional and careerist of high achievement, engages with and defines her maternal feelings, responds to a perpetually sexist and patriarchal culture, and re-configures her body and identity by fully embracing the things she most fears – most notably, the alien itself. H. R. Giger's ambiguous design of the alien and its environments as a highly sexualised and gendered yet quasi-mechanistic organism has facilitated readings in which the deep structures of the primal scene, gender orientation and sexual determinacy are played out in contradictory and ambivalent ways. However, the fundamental tension in the films remains the threat of the alien to human life, and consequently raises the key question of the genre: what is it to be human? The achievement of the films is that they transcend this question, and posit a symbolic understanding of what it is to be a woman in the contemporary world. Janice Hocker Rushing (1995) also argues of the first two films that the representation of the mother alien retrieves the myth of 'the bad mother' avenging her exploitation and relegation in patriarchal culture, only to be confronted by a patriarchally co-opted 'good mother', Ripley. Nevertheless, she suggests that the rise and impact of 'the dark goddess' and her offspring constitute an important intervention in the militarist/ bureaucratic/commercial continuum at the heart of the narratives (see Rushing 1995: 94–119; Eaton 1997; Kuhn 1990).

Animated alternatives

Some of the most powerful images in the horror genre have actually been created within the field of animation. This section, prompted mostly by the impactive apocalyptic imagery of recent Japanese manga animé, is a brief summary of some of the key texts in what may be viewed as a sub-genre of the horror film.

Although Edison's 1910 version of *Frankenstein* is often cited as the first obvious example of the genre, given its direct antecedent in Shelley's novel, a claim could be made for Winsor McCay's 1912 animation *The Story of a Mosquito* as one of the first films which depicts a genuinely monstrous creature. This comes in the guise of an outsized vampiric mosquito which constantly penetrates the skull of a sleeping man with a sharpened proboscis, drawing more and more blood into its abdomen until it explodes. Giannalberto Bendazzi (1994) suggests, however, that *The Tell-Tale Heart* (1953) was the first example of an animated horror movie. Arguably, though many cartoonal horrors preceded UPA's sophisticated Edgar Allan Poe adaptation, demonstrating the animated medium's unique vocabulary and natural affiliation to uncanny effects and supernatural movement. As early as 1906, J. Stuart Blackton's *The Haunted Hotel* demonstrates these qualities. Ladislaw Starewicz's puppet bestiary is located in the brutality and unsentimentality of the fairytale, with a claustrophobic sense of death and decay. The insects in *The Cameraman's Revenge* (1911), the rats in *Town Rat, Country Rat* (1927), and the skeletal grotesques in *The Mascot* (1923) all point to an ambivalent and destructive animality underpinning human conduct. Indeed, the cartoon *noir* aspects of the Fleischer Brothers' Betty Boop cartoons – *Minnie the Moocher* (1932) and *Betty Boop's Snow White* (1933) – also concentrate on creating a dark underworld of corruption, decadence and temptation, correspondent to the blues narratives sung in the films. The palpable sense of threat is a long way from the gothic playfulness of Disney's *The Skeleton Dance* (1929) or Van Beuren's *Wot A Night* (1931), but the wicked queen in *Snow White and the Seven Dwarfs* (1937) and the 'Night on Bald Mountain' sequence in *Fantasia* (1940) are rendered in a spirit which seeks to use the colour and fluid dynamics of the medium to illustrate the rhythm and effects of evil forces personified. In 1933 Alexander Alexeieff also made a version of *Night on Bald Mountain* (the witches' carnival on the Summer Solstice) similarly based on Mussorgsky's 1876 symphony, and suggests 'I believed I was showing the struggle between good and evil, between night and day. Much later, I discovered that I recounted the drama of my father's death and the metamorphosis of my mother who became depressed' (cited in Bendazzi 1994: 112). Complex themes also inform Nino and Toni Pagot's *The Dynamite Brothers* (1946), alluding to prison camps in a sequence set in hell.

The utopian idyll of 1930s and 1940s America was best epitomised in the animated films of the Walt Disney Studios, but mapped against these texts the horror film was a pertinent and persuasive model of the darker underbelly of American culture. This was reflected in the cartoons of other studios. Even Disney's *The Mad Doctor* (1933), a spoof of the Universal horrors, involves Pluto being kidnapped by a mad scientist and falling foul of ghosts in a gothic castle. The BBFC refused the film a certificate on the basis that it remained too frightening. Warner Bros. reference *Dr Jeckyll and Mr Hyde* in *Three's A Crowd* (1933), and mount their own, post-*Kong*, *Beauty and the Beast* in 1934, but the key motif that was taken up by animation studios was the creation of Frankenstein's monster. Interestingly, however, in the cartoon this is translated into a concern with modernist developments in industry, design and technology. In 1932 the Fleischer Brothers made *The Robot* and Walter Lantz re-released Disney's 1927 silent short *The Mechanical Cow*. A year later Ub Iwerks made *Techno-Cracked* (1933), Disney made *Mickey's Mechanical Man* (1933) and

Warner Bros. made *Bosko's Mechanical Man*. Although the cartoon inevitably sought comic events in its short narrative form, it clearly reflects the generic anxieties raised within the horror genre and science fiction literature of the period.

As noted earlier, Ray Harryhausen's work is one of the distinctive aspects of the 1950s 'creature feature' cycle, using stop-motion animation to create plausible monsters in *It Came from Beneath the Sea*, *Earth vs the Flying Saucers* and *20 Million Miles to Earth* (1957). Works in Eastern European animation during the 1960s and 1970s share the same approach to radical politics as live action counterparts like *Night of the Living Dead*, and graphically illustrate the pessimistic tone of the period. Walarian Borowczyk's *Les Jeux Des Anges* (1964) and *Théâtre de M. et Mme Kabal* (1967) use alienation devices in their imagery to create indeterminate menaces and oppressive environments emphasising the lack of humanity in post-war industrial culture. Informed by the lessons of Nazi occupation, the terrors of the concentration camps and the loss of artisan traditions, Borowczyk's films are bleak, nightmarish hallucinations.

Zagreb film-makers Aleksandar Marks and Vladimir Jutrisa's *The Fly* (1966) and *Passing Days* (1967) are similarly lacking in optimism, Kafkaesque in tone, and hold out little hope for the individual in an oppressive and chaotic universe (see Wells 1996). Animation's ability to condense, intensify and suggest themes is well illustrated in these films, but as Bendazzi suggests, it is Pavao Stalter's *Mask of the Red Death* (1969) that 'can be properly defined as a masterpiece in the genre of animated horror movies' (1994: 338). Oblique and poignant, the film shares much with Caroline Leaf's Kafka adaptation *The Metamorphosis of Mr Samsa* (1977), revealing metamorphoses and symbolic motifs that heighten the sense of paranoia, decay and hopelessness (see Wells 1999b). Although Zoran Jovanovic's *The Time of the Vampires* (1971) is more generically grounded, one of the key works of the period remains Sandor Reisenbüchler's *The Kidnapping of the Sun and the Moon* (1968), featuring a monster (the war) devouring the earth and sky, ultimately defeated by humankind. The film stands as a profound reminder of deep primal myths and their inherently human values in the face of modern warfare and the self-destructive aspects of the human race. The monster here, like many in the horror genre, is one of humankind's own making, and still subject to its understanding and correction.

Contemporary animation, as a parallel form of the horror film, has pursued a number of related themes, perhaps most notably, and inevitably, given the fluidities of the animated vocabulary, the mutability of the body and collapsing codes and conventions of social and cultural identity. Raoul Servais' *Harpya* (1978) shows a voracious and omnipresent harpy literally eating through house and home, constantly threatening its owner. The Quay brothers' *Street of Crocodiles* (1986) and *The Comb* (1990) 're-animate' detritus, reconfiguring environments, using movement in matter to illustrate the 'undead'. Jan Svankmajer engages with issues of power and status by showing the inherent and historical brutalities revealed through the animation of real objects and materials in films as diverse as *The Fall of the House of Usher* (1981), *Dimensions of Dialogue* (1982), *Down to the Cellar* (1982), *Alice* (1987), and *Faust* (1994). Furthermore, David Anderson creates an indeterminate, androgynous, apocalyptic figure in *Deadsy* (1990) and Robert Stenhouse calls upon antipodean folklore to recount the story of *The Frog, The Dog and The Devil* (1986). Victor Faccinto's *Book of Dead* (1980) remains a key expression of the ways in which animation can facilitate an aesthetically engaging but complex address of some of the taboo aspects of bodily form, violence, and the inevitability of death. It is this inevitability which has been explored in three key approaches in the animation field: intimations of the apocalypse (in films like Jimmy Murakami's *When the Wind Blows* (1986)), the clash between tradition (myth) and modernity (technology) (most notably in Japanese animation from Kihachiro Kawamoto's *The She Devil* (1972) and *Dojoji Temple* (1976) to contemporary animé such as *Legend of the Overfiend* (1989) and the postmodern angst of *Ghost in the Shell* (1995)), and finally, in the retro-playfulness of monstrosity in films as diverse as Hamburger and Fonseca's *Frankenstein Punk* (1986), Juan Padron's *Vampires in Havana* (1985) and Henry Selick's *The Nightmare Before Christmas* (1993) (for further elaboration of these themes, see Wells 1998).

Urban myths

The late twentieth-century horror film has been increasingly torn between validating its existence through extended re-workings of its established stories, or engaging with ever more realistic depictions of the known horrors of the modern world. Thus the genre constantly recycles itself through films like Francis Coppola's *Bram Stoker's Dracula* (1992), Kenneth Branagh's *Mary Shelley's Frankenstein* – both addressing the limits of the body in the AIDS era and exploring the new virility in contemporary masculinity; parodies like David Price's *Dr Jeckyll and Ms Hyde* (1995) and Mel Brooks's *Dracula: Dead and Loving It* (1995); and re-working, like Stephen Frears' Dr Jeckyll variant *Mary Reilly* (1996), and Disney's *The Hunchback of Notre Dame* (1996). While these films recirculate genre conventions in an essentially postmodern style, the more realist variations speak to another model of assumed knowledge in the contemporary audience, the urban myth. In many ways these kind of stories reconcile fantasy and reality by authenticating the source of the narrative and suggesting that, however extreme the tale, it is ostensibly 'true'. By locating the modern within the folkloric these narratives play out a tension between urbane domestic routines and 'old world' customs, sometimes bringing primitive cultures into conflict with the taken-for-granted patterns of ordered contemporary existence.

Although credible, these stories are often ambiguous and contradictory, infused to varying degrees with black humour. Their strength lies in the notion that they emerge from an oral tradition, and they gain plausibility from the historic continuum that insists that these events have actually happened. These are largely secular myths that are rooted in the cultures of lawlessness and chaos outside the safety of the law and order underpinning established social structures. They include:

– the psychopath, escaped from an asylum, often mutilated in some way and terrorising the community from which he became alienated.
– the deranged babysitter, either harming the children in her care or being threatened by an unknown phone caller, actually phoning from the very place where both reside.

FIGURE 7 *Bram Stoker's Dracula (1992)*

- the catastrophic effects of vermin and insects, often brought into an environment in innocence or by mistake.
- the unknown or accidental consumption of human flesh, vermin, insects and so on by innocent people in contexts which establish themselves as reputable and orthodox.

These examples may be readily evidenced in many sub-genres of the horror film, gaining purchase through their status as repositories for intensified experience, or what Stephen King has described as the feeling of 'revulsion', adding 'anybody who has ever discovered a spider in bed with them, or has got a bat caught in their hair knows what revulsion is'. Arguably, contemporary movies in general attempt to engage with these intensified experiences, and many call upon moments of revulsion in their texts. Films as varied as Peter Greenaway's ostensibly art-house productions *The Cook, the Thief, His Wife & Her Lover* (1990) and *The Baby of Macon* (1993), Steven Spielberg's mainstream blockbuster *Jurassic Park*

(1993) or Quentin Tarantino's *Reservoir Dogs* (1992) and *Pulp Fiction* (1994) all include shock moments and 'unusual' violent acts: forced feeding of faeces, sexual assault, bodies consumed, an ear cut off and a head blown to pieces – all previously the domain of the horror or exploitation text. Interestingly, Quentin Tarantino's ambition to find acceptance for his work amongst his peers and 'heroes' in the horror field – these including Stuart Gordon and Wes Craven – failed when some walked out of a showing of *Reservoir Dogs*. Craven argued 'I guess I'm old fashioned. I think that true horror, true suffering is appalling. I'm quite willing to do films about it, but I want to treat it seriously. I hate it when it's trivialised'.

In a sense, the more persuasive urban myth films work as a compromise between the ambivalent realist and postmodern perspectives. Bernard Rose's *Candyman* (1992), based on the Clive Barker short story 'The Forbidden', and its sequel *Candyman 2: Farewell to the Flesh* (1995), engage with the hook-handed figure of the Candyman (Tony Todd), who, in the style of the 'Mary Worth' legend, is conjured by reciting his name five times while standing in front of a mirror. The Candyman is actually the ghost of a murdered black slave, Daniel Robitaille, and his return prompts his revenge upon white, civilised society. Clearly a metaphor about racist culture and the prevailing legacy of slavery, the monster – essentially a brutal avenger – is once again morally ambivalent because of the apparent justice that motivates him. Here the arcane, primitive world perpetrates a seemingly justifiable horror which the contemporary world must confront in order to find understanding and achieve atonement. In this imperative the urban myth and the horror genre become necessary and significant models of socially relevant expression and influence.

The horror film is dead, long live the horror film

In Francis Coppola's Vietnam epic *Apocalypse Now* (1979), the deeply alienated yet visionary figure of Colonel Kurtz says 'you must make a friend of horror; horror and moral terror are your friends'. In the millenial era, it is clear that the horror text has done much to embrace the deep anxieties of modern life, and has been so influential that its conventions and ethos now underpin many contemporary mainstream films. Horror has somehow become a 'friend'; so much so that audiences can accept the bleak ending of *Se7en* (1995), which refuses any notion of redemption from its apocalyptic tale of fundamentalist obsession involving the sacrificial killings of figures who are the symbolic embodiment of the seven deadly sins. This is a mature vision which recognises that audiences have come to terms with the darkness at the heart of contemporary civilisation and can endure its less palatable outcomes. One of the reasons that this is so is due to the role of the horror film in rehearsing the deepest of fears and visualising our worst nightmares. In living through these fictions, it is possible to live through the vicissisitudes of experience at its most extreme. Perhaps, in the 'replica' re-make of *Psycho* (1998) there is an acknowledgement that there is nothing more to say, but still much to be learned from the genre. As Clive Barker suggests, 'our fears can only be addressed in the language of the dream, and horror fiction gives us that vocabulary, and helps our conscious mind confront anxiety and shape our world view. Understanding fear is part of us, and must be embraced'.

In a contemporary world where there are few shared and common knowledges, the nursery rhyme, the fairytale, and the folktale, and their contemporary counterpart, the horror movie, still provide a context in which everyone shares the same language. Jenny Diski believes that 'civilisation may be the art of looking away, but there have always been some who choose to look directly at the darkness simply because the truth is that monsters are always with us, very near' (1992: 35). In the light of Diski's statement, it becomes clear that the horror film will always survive if it can find ways of 'looking directly into the darkness', finding modes of expression which re-define the codes and conventions of the genre, and in so doing foreground the primal fears inherent in the narratives rather than the generic motifs that have traditionally expressed them. The already legendary *The Blair Witch Project* (1999) emphatically succeeds in doing this by essentially recovering 'suggestion' and 'allusion' in the horror film, and with them the idea that the most persuasive horror is the one suggested in the mind of the viewer, rather than that which is explicitly expressed on the screen. Crucially, this has been achieved by using the new technologies that have become available as mainstream vehicles of recording and expression; most obviously, the video camera and the personal computer. The audience now has a clear understanding of both the aesthetic look of video imagery, and the extraordinary capabilities of the world wide web in regard to the creation of a flow of information to interested parties across the world. It is in embracing this knowledge that directors Daniel Myrick and Eduardo Sanchez have significantly progressed the genre.

The film's premise, that this is a movie assembled from documentary 'actuality' footage found at Burkittsville, Maryland, by 'Haxan Films', a small production company, immediately seems to blur the line between fact and fiction. Three student film-makers who are undertaking research about a legendary witch and a number of unsolved child murders in the region many years before have filmed this material but are now missing, presumed dead. This then is 'amateur' footage, seemingly shot with inexperienced eyes and limited technique, and thus, ironically, possessing greater veracity and authenticity in its verité approach. Whatever the audience sees, it is suggested, actually happened. Shot from the point-of-view of the characters, it offers no objective place for the viewer to watch their experiences from.

Myrick and Sanchez have created a text in which no one participant or viewer is quite certain of the status of the events that are occurring. This is partly due to the pragmatic necessities of making a film on a $30,000 budget, and partly due to the 'guerilla' style approach to actually making the film; for example, creating narrative events where the actors are improvising within a scenario, but are *genuinely* frightened by what they unknowingly encounter. Although the actors in the film – Heather Donahue, Joshua Leonard and Michael Williams – know that they are participating in a fiction, their real emotions and fears are exploited through the way that the film is made, thus enhancing the veracity of the horror the viewer is asked to imagine in the story they witness. This is further authenticated by the back story of the 'Blair Witch' legend that appeared on a web site preceding the film. This is a sophisticated piece of publicity for the film, functioning, in advance of the film's distribution, as a folk-legend that passed into popular culture as 'true'. The film creates and maintains its effect because the directors sustain the ambivalent play of fact and fiction both about the making of, and the content within, the film and its supporting contexts of supplementary information.

Although the influence of fairytales like 'Hansel and Gretel' and films like Peter Weir's *Picnic at Hanging Rock* (1975) are clear, this film is basically a return to a method approach to acting and film-making, where there is a commitment to as realistic a portrayal of emotions and events as possible. The heightened naturalism of *The Blair Witch Project* coherently underpins the 'instability' of the supernatural environment. Those who apparently start out in control soon become victims of events which cannot be circumscribed back within the safe parameters of known facts. The fundamental and primal fear experienced by the actors/characters is then re-inscribed as the way in which the film-makers can also prevent the audience from returning to the safe parameters of generic expectation. Again, the web site, with its moving palette of additional footage, interviews and documents, reinforces this, and draws upon the known 'obsessiveness' of the net-freaks and genre fans who serve to believe in, perpetuate and extend the mythology. 'Word of mouse' significantly enhances the credentials of the film and authenticates the idea that the viewer is *within* a world, not *observing* one, and that this kind of horror is about personal dread rather than a shared knowledge of motifs and generic norms. A supporting promotional film, *Curse of the Blair Witch*, in echoing the film's approach and by using materials that appeared on the web site, refuses an 'exit' from the circuit of publicity/authentication for the overall text.

The Last Broadcast (1998) shares many of the characteristics of *The Blair Witch Project* in style, content, and supplementary internet material. While there may be some small debate about the nature of the similarity, the presence of such independent yet impactive films, in re-defining the approach to the thriller/horror formula by directly interacting with their potential audiences on-line, is a significant development. It is also 'virtual' evidence of a late-millenial *zeitgeist* which is still preoccupied with mortality. If the treatment of young people and children within recent slasher movies, and the knowing irony accorded to its youth audience, was merely superficial in its representation of death and disorder, it is perhaps the case that the *fin-de-siècle* concerns for the future of the young have become more pronounced and serious. *The Sixth Sense* (1999), *Stir of Echoes* (1999) and *Stigmata* (1999) share this anxiety, and all use the supernatural and the realm of superstition as vehicles to express the view that although we have progressed in the twentieth century, there is still much beyond our comprehension as we enter the twenty-first. Humanity, although enhanced by its technologies and cultural sophistication, has not really advanced, and stripped of its material accessories – as in *The Blair Witch Project* – still suffers deep anxiety about the tenuous nature of existence and the lack of what may be viewed as spiritual purpose. The horror film has done much to draw us back to this issue, and in heightening our consciousness to our vulnerable status, and reminding us that 'fear' can protect us, insists that it is fundamental in our view of ourselves and the value of life.

Wes Craven suggests 'we have created a world where we can only be perceived as mature and "realistic" if we have left behind our innocence. This is terrible, of course, some might say cynical, but all the truer if we see that this is the very point the horror movie wishes us to constantly confront'. This view readily chimes with the childhood recollection of Clive Barker, who witnessed the death of 'Birdman' Leo Valentin, when the aerial performer's parachute failed to open following a flying stunt. It is also a fitting conclusion to this discussion:

I'm looking out of the car window, and there, at the edge of the cornfield, stand my father and uncle, watching the last moments of the Birdman's fall. No doubt they were as panicked as everyone else, but that's not how I remember them. What I picture in my mind's eye are two stoic witnesses to this terrible scene. This was maleness, this witnessing; or so in that moment I came to believe. And if my work is marked by a certain hunger to see what should not be seen, to show what should not be shown, the beginning of that appetite may be here, at the edge of the cornfield with the men watching the key, and me, struggling in my mother's arms because I was forbidden the sight.

NOTES

1 Interview with the author. Unless otherwise stated, cited quotations with directors, actors, practitioners and so on hereafter are drawn from interviews with the author which took place between September 1992 and June 1995.

2 Other works by Freud which impact upon aspects of the study of the horror genre are available as part of the Pelican Freud Library and relevant volumes in the series include: Volume 4: *The Interpretation of Dreams*, Volume 12: *Civilisation, Society and Religion* and Volume 14: *Art and Literature*.

3 Some useful, entertaining, and pertinent web sites engaged with the horror genre may be found at the following addresses:

   http://www.webcom.com/tby/cbarker.html
   http://www.filmscouts.com
   http://guest.binterest.com/~revelations/
   http://horrorfilms.8m.com
   http://www.pe.net/~karloff/
   http://www.auracom.com/~tournier/webworld.htm
   http://www.acm.vt.edu/~yousten/lewton/index.html
   http://www.stephenking.com
   http://www.blairwitch.com

GLOSSARY

Definitions given here are related to the specific use made of these terms in their place of appearance in the text.

body horror
The explicit display of the decay, dissolution or destruction of the body, foregrounding bodily processes and functions under threat, allied to new physiological configurations and re-definitions of anatomical norms.

camp
An approach to representation which foregrounds the ironic, and often exaggerated 'performance' of certain gender positions, sexual orientations and social identities, challenging previous cultural and historical orthodoxies.

carnivalesque
The excessive celebration of the temporary reversal and revision of social orthodoxy, privileging often taboo forms of human expression and the primacy of bodily functions.

censorship
The process by which particular kinds of textual or visual material may be acted upon, altered or forbidden publication, distribution or broadcast by regulators, working within legally determined guidelines which assume particular codes and limits to public consumption.

Creature Feature
A cycle of largely B-movie films made in the United States during the 1950s which feature a whole range of prehistoric, alien or imagined monsters who terrorise big cities.

Expressionism
An artistic movement privileging a non-realist approach to symbolic forms of design reflecting interior states of mind and extreme emotions.

gore
The excessive display of bodily organs in a state of bloodied transition or exposure.

Grand Guignol
A highly theatrical, melodramatic style of performance, which foregrounds sadistic and apparently 'live' horror effects like eye-gouging, stabbing and hanging.

incoherent cinema
Rather than being a negative comment, this is a mode of cinema which works to challenge the dominant characteristics of classical Hollywood narrative, using the camera or the editing process to draw the audience's attention to other possibilities in the narrative or in the aesthetic use of the medium. This often leads to quite surreal and arbitrary effects which almost demand that the audience watch 'cinema' for its own sake, rather than get drawn into 'storytelling' or other kinds of visual orthodoxy which have come to characterise film-making practice.

metamorphosis
The fluid evolution from one state to another, exhibiting the protean process of a form. This can be a physical state, as it is often expressed through transition and transformation in the monster, or a technical process, as illustrated within the animated form as one image evolves into another without the necessity of edit.

modernism
The 'modernist' period has been subject to much debate and contention. Some argue that modernism as a period of social change may be traced from the building of the Eiffel Tower in Paris in 1896 right through to the end of the Second World War in 1945. For the purposes of this discussion, modernism is perceived as the logical consequence of the social, political, philosophical and scientific thought of the mid-nineteenth century as it translated into the new communications era of the twentieth century.

revenge of nature
A range of horror films based on the idea that the everyday things that humankind take for granted in nature – the complicity of insects, animals and birds; the predictable growth of flowers and vegetables; the elemental and seasonal cycles and so on – will one day cease to operate in the anticipated manner, and inexplicably 'rise' to take its revenge on the exploitation and insensitivity of human beings.

serial killer
A comparitively modern phenomenon in a which an individual commits a series of related, often ritualistic murders, while sometimes courting a symbiotic relationship with the authorities and the media who are attempting to apprehend him.

FILMOGRAPHY

Note: Different sources often give differing dates for the same film, a confusion arising from the fact that some use the date of production, while others give the year of release in one country or another. For the sake of consistency we have used a single source, the Internet Movie DataBase (www.us.imdb.com), which uses the date of release, usually in the United States.

Alice (Jan Svankmajer, 1987, Switz./Ger./UK)
Alien (Ridley Scott, 1979, UK)
Alien³ (David Fincher, 1992, US)
Alien Resurrection (Jean-Pierre Jeunet, 1997, US)
Aliens (James Cameron, 1986, US)
All the President's Men (Alan Pakula, 1976, US)
Apocalypse Now (Francis Ford Coppola, 1979, US)
Attack of the Fifty Foot Woman (Nathan Juran, 1958, US)
Avenging Conscience, The (D. W. Griffith, 1914, US)
Awful Dr Orloff, The (Jesus Franco, 1962, Sp.)
Baby of Macon, The (Peter Greenaway, 1993, UK/Neth./Fr./Ger.)
Bad Seed, The (Mervyn LeRoy, 1956, US)
Bare-Chested Countess, The (Jesus Franco, 1975, Bel./Fr.)
Baron of Terror ('Barón del terror, El') (Chano Ureta, 1961, Mex.)
Basic Instinct (Paul Verhoeven, 1992, US)
Basket Case (Frank Henenlotter, 1982, US)
Batman Returns (Tim Burton, 1992, US)
Bay of Blood, A ('Reazione a catena') (Mario Bava, 1971, It.)
Beast from 20,000 Fathoms, The (Eugne Louri,1953, US)
Beauty and the Beast (Fritz Freleng, 1934, US)
Bedlam (Mark Robson, 1946, US)
Behemoth, the Sea Monster (Douglas Hickox, Eugne Louri, 1959, UK)

Betty Boop's Snow White (Dave Fleischer, 1933, US)

Beyond, The ('. . . E Tu Vivrai nel Terrore! L'Aldila') (Lucio Fulci, 1981, It.)

Birds, The (Alfred Hitchcock, 1963, US)

Black Cat, The (aka *House of Doom*) (Edgar Ulmer, 1934, US)

Blackmail (Alfred Hitchcock, 1929, UK)

Black Room, The (Roy William Neill, 1935, US)

Black Sunday ('Maschera del Demonio, La') (aka *Mask of the Demon*) (Mario Bava, 1960, It.)

Blair Witch Project, The (Daniel Myrick, Eduardo Sanchez, 1999, US)

Blind Bargain, A (Wallace Worsley, 1922, US)

Blood Feast (Herschell Gordon Lewis, 1963, US)

Blue Demon Versus the Infernal Brains ('Cerebro Infernal') (Chano Urueto, 1967, Mex.)

Body Snatcher, The (Robert Wise, 1945, US)

Bodysnatcher (1956)

Book of Dead (Victor Faccinto, 1980, US)

Bosko's Mechanical Man (Hugh Harmon, 1933, US)

Bram Stoker's Dracula (Francis Ford Coppola, 1992, US)

Bride of Frankenstein, The (James Whale, 1935, US)

Brood, The (David Cronenberg, 1979, Can.)

Cabinet of Dr Caligari, The ('Das Kabinett des Dr Caligari') (Robert Wiene, 1919, Ger.)

Cameraman's Revenge, The (Wladyslaw Starewicz, 1911, Rus.)

Candyman (Bernard Rose, 1992, US)

Candyman 2: Farewell to the Flesh (Bill Condon, 1995, US)

Cannibal ('Ultimo Mondo Cannibale') (Ruggero Deodato, 1976, It.)

Cannibal Ferox (Umberto Lenzi, 1980, It.)

Cannibal Holocaust (Ruggero Deodato, 1979, It.)

Cannibals (Jesus Franco, 1979, Sp.)

Carrie (Brian De Palma, 1976, US)

Cat People (Jacques Tourneur, 1942, US)

Cat People (Paul Schrader, 1982, US)

Child's Play 3 (Jack Bender, 1991, US)

Circus of Horrors (Sidney Hayers, 1960, UK)

Colossus of New York, The (Eugne Louri, 1958, US)

Comb, The (Stephen Quay, Timothy Quay, 1990, UK)

Company of Wolves, The (Neil Jordan, 1984, UK)

Conversation, The (Francis Ford Coppola, 1974, US)

Cook, the Thief, His Wife & Her Lover, The (Peter Greenaway, 1990, UK)

Copycat (Jon Amiel, 1995, US)

Count Yorga, Vampire (Bob Kelljan, 1970, US)

Crash (David Cronenberg, 1996, Can.)

Creature from the Black Lagoon (Jack Arnold, 1954, US)

Creature Walks Among Us, The (John Sherwood, 1956, US)

Crying Woman, The (Rafael Baledón, 1933, Mex.)

Curse of Frankenstein, The (Terence Fisher, 1957, UK)

Curse of the Blair Witch (Daniel Myrick, Eduardo Sanchez, 1999, US)
Curse of the Cat People, The (Robert Wise, 1944, US)
Dance of the Vampires (aka *The Fearless Vampire Killers*) (Roman Polanski, 1967, US)
Dawn of the Dead (aka *Zombies*) (George Romero, 1978, US/It.)
Day of the Dead (George Romero, 1985, US)
Day the Earth Stood Still, The (Robert Wise, 1951, US)
Dead of Night (Alberto Cavalcanti, Charles Crichton, 1945, UK)
Dead Ringers (David Cronenberg, 1988, Can)
Deadsy (David Anderson, 1990, US)
Demons of the Mind (Peter Sykes, 1971, UK)
Devils, The (Ken Russell, 1971, UK)
Devil's Assistant, The (Harry Pollard, 1917, US)
Devil-Doll, The (Todd Browning, 1936, US)
Dimensions of Dialogue ('Moznosti dialogu') (Jan Svankmajer, 1982, Cz.)
Dojoji Temple ('Kyokanoko musume Dojoji') (Kihachiro Kawamoto, 1976, Jap.)
Down to the Cellar ('Do piunice') (Jan Svankmajer, 1982, Cz.)
Dr Jekyll and Mr Hyde (Rouben Mamoulian, 1931, US)
Dr Jekyll and Ms Hyde (David Price, 1995, US)
Dracula (Todd Browning, 1931, US)
Dracula: Dead and Loving It (Mel Brooks, 1995, US)
Dracula's Daughter (Lambert Hillyer, 1936, US)
Dressed to Kill (Brian De Palma, 1980, US)
Driller Killer, The (Abel Ferrara, 1979, US)
Dynamite Brothers, The (Nino and Toni Pagot, 1946, It.)
Earth vs The Flying Saucers (aka *Invasion of the Flying Saucers*) (Fred Sears, 1956, US)
Edward Scissorhands (Tim Burton, 1990, US)
Ed Wood (Tim Burton, 1994, US)
El Topo (Alexandro Jodorowsky, 1971, Mex.)
Evil Dead, The (Sam Raimi, 1982, US)
Exorcist, The (Willaim Friedkin, 1973, US)
Fall of the House of Usher, The (aka *The House of Usher*) (Roger Corman, 1960, US)
Fall of the House of Usher, The ('Zanik domu usheru') (Jan Svankmajer, 1981, Cz.)
Fantasia (James Algar, Samuel Armstrong, Ben Sharpsteen, 1940, US)
Fatal Attraction (Adrian Lyne, 1987, US)
Faust (Jan Svankmajer, 1994, UK/Fr./Cz./Ger.)
Florentine Dagger, The (Robert Florey, 1935, US)
Fly, The (Kurt Neumann, 1958, US)
Fly, The (Aleksandar Marks, Vladimir Jutrisa, 1966, Yu.)
Fly, The (David Cronenberg, 1986, US)
Frankenstein (J. Searle Dawley, 1910, US)
Frankenstein (James Whale, 1931, US)
Frankenstein Meets the Wolf Man (Roy William Neill, 1946, US)
Frankenstein Punk (Eliana Fonseca, Cao Hamburger, 1986, Braz.)

Freaks (Tod Browning, 1932, US)

Freddy's Dead: The Final Nightmare (Rachel Talalay, 1990, US)

Friday the 13th (Sean Cunningham, 1980, US)

Friday the 13th Part 2 (Steve Miner, 1981, US)

Friday the 13th Part 3: 3D (Steve Miner, 1982, Can./US)

Friday the 13th Part V: A New Beginning (Danny Steinmann, 1985, US)

Friday the 13th Part VI: Jason Lives (Tom McLoughlin, 1986, US)

Friday the 13th Part VII: The New Blood (John Carl Buechler, 1988, US)

Friday the 13th Part VIII: Jason Takes Manhattan (Rob Hedden, 1989, US)

Friday the 13th: The Final Chapter (Joseph Zito, 1984, US)

Frightmare (Pete Walker, 1974, UK)

Frog, the Dog, and the Devil, The (Robert Stenhouse, 1986, NZ)

Fury, The (Brian De Palma, 1978, US)

Ghost in the Shell ('Kokaku Kidotai') (Mamoru Oshii, 1995, Jap./UK)

Gods and Monsters (Bill Condon, 1998, UK/US)

Godzilla ('Gojira') (Ishirô Honda, 1954, Jap./US)

Godzilla (Roland Emmerich, 1998, US)

Gold Diggers of 1933, The (Mervyn LeRoy, 1933, US)

Golem, The ('Der Golem, wie er in die Welt kam') (Paul Wegener, 1920, Ger.)

Gothic (Ken Russell, 1986, UK)

Graduation Day (Herb Freed, 1981, US)

Halloween (John Carpenter, 1978, US)

Halloween II (Rick Rosenthal, 1981, US)

Hand that Rocks the Cradle, The (Curtis Hanson, 1992, US)

Hands of Orlac, The (aka *Mad Love*) (Karl Freund, 1935, US)

Harpya (Raoul Servais, 1978, Sp.)

Haunted Hotel, The (J. Stuart Blackton, 1906, US)

Hellraiser (Clive Barker, 1987, US)

Hellraiser II: Hellbound (Tony Randel, 1988, UK)

Hellraiser IV: Bloodline (Kevin Yagher, 1996, US)

Hellraiser III: Hell on Earth (Anthony Hickox, 1992, US)

Henry, Portrait of a Serial Killer (John McNaughton, 1986, US)

Horrors of the Black Museum (Arthur Crabtree, 1959, UK)

Hound of the Baskervilles (Sidney Lanfield, 1939, US)

Hounds of Zaroff, The (aka *The Most Dangerous Game*) (Ernest Schoedsack, 1932, US)

House on the Haunted Hill (William Castle, 1958, US)

House of Wax (André de Toth, 1953, US)

Human Wreckage (John Griffith Wray, 1923, US)

Hunchback of Notre Dame, The (William Dieterle, 1939, US)

Hunchback of Notre Dame, The (Gary Trousdale, 1996, US)

Hunger, The (Tony Scott, 1983, US)

I Know What You Did Last Summer (Jim Gillespie, 1997, US)

I Married a Monster From Outer Space (Gene Fowler, 1958, US)

I Spit on your Grave (aka *Day of the Woman*) (Meir Zarchi, 1978, US)
I Walked with a Zombie (Jacques Tourneur, 1943, US)
I Was a Teenage Frankenstein (Herbert Strock, 1957, US)
I Was a Teenage Werewolf (Gene Fowler, 1957, US)
Incredible Shrinking Man, The (Jack Arnold, 1957, US)
Inferno (Dario Argento, 1980, It.)
Interview With the Vampire (Neil Jordan, 1994, US)
Invasion of the Body Snatchers (Don Siegel, 1956, US)
Invisible Ray, The (Lambert Hillyer, 1936, US)
Isle of the Dead (Mark Robson, 1945, US)
It Came From Beneath The Sea (Robert Gordon, 1955, US)
It Happened One Night (Frank Capra, 1934, US)
It Lives Again (Larry Cohen, 1978, US)
It's Alive! (Larry Cohen, 1973, US)
It's Alive III: Island of the Alive (Larry Cohen, 1987, US)
It's Always Fair Weather (Stanley Donen, Gene Kelly, 1955, US)
Jason Goes to Hell: The Final Friday (Adam Marcus, 1993, US)
Jaws (Steven Spielberg, 1975, US)
Jurassic Park (Steven Spielberg, 1993, US)
Kidnapping of the Sun and the Moon, The (Sandor Reisenbüchler, 1968, Hun.)
King Kong (Merian Cooper, Ernest Schoedsack, 1933, US)
Lair of the White Worm, The (Ken Russell, 1988, UK)
Last Broadcast, The (Stephan Avalos, Lance Weiler, 1998, US)
Last House on the Left, The (aka *Krug and Company*) (Wes Craven, 1972, US)
Legend of the Overfiend ('Chôjin denstsu urotsukidôji') (Hideki Takayama, 1989, Jap.)
Leopard Man, The (Jacques Tourneur, 1943, US)
Lesbian Vampires, The (Jesus Franco, 1970, Sp./Ger.)
Les Jeux Des Anges ('The Game of the Angels') (Walerian Borowczyk, 1964, Fr.)
London After Midnight (Tod Browning, 1927, US)
Lost Highway (David Lynch, 1997, US)
Lost Horizon (Frank Capra, 1937, US)
Lust for a Vampire (Jimmy Sangster, 1971, UK)
Lust of the Vampire ('Vampiri, I') (Riccardo Freda, 1956, It.)
Lost Boys, The (Joel Schumacher, 1987, US)
Lost Horizon (Frank Capra, 1937, US)
Macabre (William Castle, 1958, US)
Mad Doctor, The (David Hand, 1933, US)
Mad Monster Party (Jules Bass, 1967, US)
Mahakaal (Tutsi and Shyam Ramsay, 1994, Ind.)
Marathon Man (John Schlesinger, 1976, US)
Mark of the Vampire (Tod Browning, 1935, US)
Mary Reilly (Stephen Frears, 1996, US)
Mary Shelley's Frankenstein (Kenneth Branagh, 1994, UK)

Mascot, The ('Fétiche') (Wladyslaw Starewicz, 1923, Fr.)
Mask of Fu Manchu, The (Charles Brabin, 1932, US)
Mask of the Red Death (Pavao Stalter, 1969, Yu.)
Masque of the Red Death, The (Roger Corman, 1964, UK)
Mechanical Cow, The (Walt Disney, 1927, US)
Metamorphosis of Mr Samsa, The (Caroline Leaf, 1977, Can.)
Mickey's Mechanical Man (Wilfred Jackson, 1933, US)
Minnie the Moocher (Dave Fleischer, 1932, US)
Misery (Rob Reiner, 1990, US)
Mondo Cane (aka *A Dog's Life*) (Gualtiero Jacopetti, Franco Prosperi, 1963, It.)
Monster from the Ocean Floor (Wyott Ordung, 1954, US)
Monster that Challenged the World, The (Arnold Laven, 1957, US)
Mr Deeds Goes to Town (Frank Capra, 1936, US)
Mr Smith Goes to Washington (Frank Capra, 1939, US)
Mystery of the Pallid Face, The (Juan Bustillo Oro, 1934, Mex.)
Naked Lunch (David Cronenberg, 1991, UK/Can.)
Near Dark (Kathryn Bigelow, 1987, US)
Necronomicon (Jesus Franco, 1967, Sp.)
Night of the Living Dead (George Romero, 1968, US)
Night on Bald Mountain ('Une nuit sur le mont chauve') (Alexander Alexeieff, Clare Parker, 1933, Fr.)
Nightmare Before Christmas, The (Tim Burton, 1993, US)
Nightmare on Elm Street, A (Wes Craven, 1984, US)
Nightmare on Elm Street Part 3: Dream Warriors, A (Chuck Russell, 1987, US)
Nightmare on Elm Street Part 2: Freddy's Revenge, A (Jack Sholder, 1985, US)
Nightmare on Elm Street Part 5: The Dream Child, A (Stephen Hopkins, 1989, US)
Nightmare on Elm Street Part 4: The Dream Master, A (Renny Harlin, 1988, US)
Nosferatu, eine Symphonie des Grauens (Nosferatu the Vampire) (F. W. Murnau, 1922, Ger.)
Old Dark House, The (James Whale, 1932, US)
Omen, The (Richard Donner, 1976, US)
On the Town (Stanley Donen, Gene Kelly, 1949, US)
On the Waterfront (Elia Kazan, 1954, US)
Parallax View, The (Alan Pakula, 1974, US)
Parents (Bob Balaban, 1989, US)
Passing Days (Aleksandar Marks, Vladimir Jutrisa, 1967, Yu.)
Peeping Tom (Michael Powell, 1960, UK)
People Under the Stairs, The (Wes Craven, 1992, US)
Phantom of the Convent, The (Fernando de Fuentes, 1934, Mex.)
Phantom of the Opera, The (Rupert Julian, 1925, US)
Phantom of the Paradise (Brian De Palma, 1974, US)
Picnic at Hanging Rock (Peter Weir, 1975, Aus.)
Pit and the Pendulum, The (Roger Corman, 1961, US)
Planet of the Vampires ('Terrore nello spazio') (Mario Bava, 1965, It./Sp.)

Poltergeist (Tobe Hooper, 1982, US)
Premature Burial, The (Roger Corman, 1962, US)
Psycho (Alfred Hitchcock, 1960, US)
Psycho (Gus Van Sant, 1998, US)
Psycho II (Richard Franklin, 1983, US)
Pulp Fiction (Quentin Tarantino, 1994, US)
Purani Haveli (Tutsi and Shyam Ramsay, 1989, Ind.)
Quatermass Xperiment, The (Val Guest, 1955, UK)
Rabid (David Cronenberg, 1976, Can.)
Rear Window (Alfred Hitchcock, 1954, US)
Re-Animator (Stuart Gordon, 1985, US)
Rebecca (Alfred Hitchcock, 1940, US)
Repulsion (Romana Polanski, 1965, UK)
Reservoir Dogs (Quentin Tarantino, 1992, US)
Return of Dracula, The (aka *The Fantastic Disappearing Man*) (Paul Landres, 1958, US)
Revenge of Frankenstein, The (Terence Fisher, 1958, UK)
Revenge of the Creature (Jack Arnold, 1955, US)
Robot, The (Dave Fleischer, 1932, US)
Rocky Horror Picture Show, The (Jim Sharman, 1975, UK)
Rosemary's Baby (Roman Polanski, 1968, US)
Sabotage (Alfred Hitchcock, 1936, UK)
Sadomania (Jesus Franco, 1980, Sp.)
Samson vs the Vampire Women ('Santo contra las mujeres vampiros, El') (Alfonso Corona Blake, 1961, Mex.)
Sante Sangre (Alejandro Jodorowsky, 1989, It.)
Scanners (David Cronenberg, 1980, Can.)
Scream (Wes Craven, 1996, US)
Sentinel, The (Michael Winner, 1977, US)
Se7en (David Fincher, 1995, US)
Seventh Victim, The (Mark Robson, 1943, US)
Shadow of a Doubt (Alfred Hitchcock, 1943, US)
She-Devil, The (Kihachiro Kawamoto, 1972, Jap.)
Shining, The (Stanley Kubrick, 1980, UK)
Shivers (*Parasite Murders, The*) (David Cronenberg, 1975, Can.)
Silence of the Lambs (Jonathan Demme, 1991, US)
Single White Female (Barbet Schroeder, 1992, US)
Sisters (aka *Blood Sisters*) (Brian De Palma, 1973, US)
Sixth Sense, The (M. Night Shyamalan, 1999, US)
Skeleton Dance, The (Ub Iwerks, 1929, US)
Sleeping With the Enemy (Joseph Ruben, 1991, US)
Snow White and the Seven Dwarfs (Walt Disney, 1937, US)
Society (Brian Yuzna, 1989, US)
Son Of Frankenstein (Rowland Lee, 1939, US)

Sorrows of Satan, The (D. W. Griffiths, 1926, US)
Space Children, The (Jack Arnold, 1958, US)
Stepfather, The (Joseph Ruben, 1986, US)
Stephen King's Thinner (Tom Holland, 1996, US)
Stigmata (Rupert Wainwright, 1999, US)
Stir of Echoes (David Koepp, 1999, US)
Story of a Mosquito, The (aka *How a Mosquito Operates*) (Winsor McCay, 1912, US)
Strangers on a Train (Alfred Hitchcock, 1951, US)
Street of Crocodiles (Stephen Quay, Timothy Quay, 1986, UK)
Suspicion (Alfred Hitchcock, 1941, US)
Suspiria (Dario Argento, 1976, It.)
Tales of Terror (Roger Corman, 1962, US)
Taxi Driver (Martin Scorcese, 1976, US)
Techno-Cracked (Ub Iwerks, 1933, US)
Tell-Tale Heart, The (Art Babbitt, Ted Parmelee, 1953, US)
Terror of Dr Hichcock, The ('L'orrible segreto del dottor Hichcock') (Riccardo Freda, 1962, It.)
Texas Chainsaw Massacre, The (Tobe Hooper, 1974, US)
Théâtre de M. et Mme Kabal (Walerian Borowczyk, 1967, Fr.)
Them! (Gordon Douglas, 1954, US)
Thing from Another World, The (Christian Nyby, 1951, US)
Three's a Crowd (Rudolf Ising, 1933, US)
Time of the Vampires, The (Zoran Jovanovic, 1971, Yu.)
Tingler, The (William Castle, 1959, US)
Toll of Mammon, The (Harry Handworth, 1914, US)
Tomb of Ligeia, The (Roger Corman, 1965, UK)
Tombs of the Blind Dead (Amando de Ossorio, 1971, Sp./Port.)
Topo, El ('The Mole') (Alejandro Jodorowsky, 1970, Mex.)
Town Rat, Country Rat (Wladyslaw Starewicz, 1927, Fr.)
Toxic Avenger, The (Michael Herz, Lloyd Kaufman, 1985, US)
Twins of Evil (John Hough, 1971, UK)
Unlawful Entry (Jonathan Kaplan, 1992, US)
Vampire, The (Paul Landres, 1957, US)
Vampire, The ('El Vampiro') (Fernando Mndez, 1957, Mex.)
Vampire and the Ballerina, The ('L'amate del vampiro') (Renato Polselli, 1959, It.)
Vampire Bat, The (Frank Strayer, 1933, US)
Vampires in Havana ('Vampiros en La Habana') (Juan Padron, 1985, Cub./Sp./Ger.)
Vampire Lovers, The (Roy Ward Baker, 1970, UK)
Vampyr (Carl Theodor Dreyer, 1932, Ger./Fr.)
Vertigo (Alfred Hitchcock, 1958, US)
Videodrome (David Cronenberg, 1982, Can.)
Werewolf's Shadow, The (Leon Klimovsky, 1970, Sp./Ger.)
Wes Craven's New Nightmare (Wes Craven, 1994, US)
When the Wind Blows (Jimmy Murakami, 1986, UK)

SHORT CUTS

White Zombie (Victor Halperin, 1932, US)
Witchfinder General (Michael Reeves, 1968, UK)
Wot a Night (John Foster, Vernon Stallings, 1931, US)
42nd Street (Lloyd Bacon, 1933, US)
20 Million Miles to Earth (Nathan Juran, 1957, US)

BIBLIOGRAPHY

The bibliography lists works cited in the text and is also designed to point to useful further reading. The annotated list of 'essential reading' highlights works considered to be of particular importance to contemporary understandings of science fiction cinema, although many valuable contributions are also to be found under 'secondary reading'.

ESSENTIAL READING

Benshoff, H. (1996) *Monsters in the Closet: Homosexuality and the Horror Film*. Manchester and New York: Manchester University Press.
  Useful engagement with gay and lesbian issues in horror films and 'queer' readings drawn from the ambivalence in many horror texts in relation to gender, sex and sexuality.
Botting, F. (1996) *Gothic*. London and New York: Routledge.
  Excellent introductory overview of the evolution, development and key preoccupations of gothic literature.
Clover, C. (1992) *Men, Women and Chainsaws: Gender in the Modern Horror Film*. New Jersey: Princeton University Press.
  Key address of the role of gender in the horror film, paying special attention to the significant role women have played as victims and provocateurs.
Creed, B. (1993) *The Monstrous Feminine: Film, Feminism & Psychoanalysis*. London and New York: Routledge.
  Incisive and often complex psychoanalytic reading of the horror film defining the 'monster' within the frame of femininity and feminism.
Hutchings, P. (1993) *Hammer and Beyond: The British Horror Film*. Manchester and New York: Manchester University Press.
  Instructive overview of the key agendas in Hammer and other British horror films and their relationship to British culture.
Jankovich, M. (1996) *Rational Fears: American Horror in the 1950s*. Manchester and New York: Manchester University Press.

Excellent reading of B-movie sci-fi/horror movies in 1950s America, exposing the preoccupations and anxieties of the post-war period within their political and social context.

Newman, K. (1988) *Nightmare Movies*. London: Bloomsbury.

Definitive introduction to contemporary horror by a leading figure in the field.

Paul, W. (1994) *Laughing, Screaming: Modern Hollywood Horror and Comedy*. New York: Columbia University Press.

Pertinent examination of the relationship between horror and humour in contemporary 'youth excess' movies.

Tudor, A. (1989) *Monsters and Mad Scientists*. Oxford and Cambridge, Massachusetts: Blackwell.

Statistically driven, sociologically informed treatise on the presence and position of 'the monster' across the history of the genre.

Wood, R. & R. Lippe (eds) (1979) *American Nightmare: Essays on the Horror Film*. Toronto: Festival of Festivals.

Seminal readings of some of the key agendas in horror texts.

SECONDARY READING

Aristotle (1920) *On the Art of Poetry*. Oxford and London: Oxford University Press.

Auerbach, N. (1997) *Our Vampires, Ourselves*. Chicago: University of Chicago Press.

Babuta, S. and J. C. Bragard (1985) *Evil*. London: Weidenfeld and Nicholson.

Bailey, L. (1996) *Film, Horror and the Body Fantastic*. Westport and London: Greenwood Press.

Bakhtin, M. (1984) *Rabelais and his World*. Bloomington and Indiana: Indiana University Press.

Barker, C. (1987) *Books of Blood Volume One*. London: HarperCollins.

Barker, C. (1999) *The Essential Barker*. London: HarperCollins.

Barker, M. (ed.) (1984) *The Video Nasties: Freedom and Censorship in the Media*. London: Pluto Press.

—— (1984) *A Haunt of Fears: The Strange History of the British Horror Comics Campaign*. London: Pluto Press.

Bataille, G. (1962) *Death and Sensuality*. New York: Walker.

Beeler, M. (1994) 'Clive Barker: Horror Visionary' in *Cinefantastique*, 26, 3, 16–44.

Berenstein, R. (1996) *Attack of the Leading Ladies: Gender, Sexuality and Spectatorship in Classic Horror Cinema*. New York: Columbia University Press.

Bettelheim, B. (1978) *The Uses of Enchantment: The Meaning and Importance of Fairytales*. London and New York: Penguin Books.

Biskind, P. (1983) *Seeing is Believing*. London and New York: Pluto Press.

Black, A. (ed.) (1996) *Necronomicon Book 1*. London: Creation.

—— (ed.) (1997) *Necronomicon Book 2*. London: Creation.

Black, J. (1991) *The Aesthetics of Murder*. Baltimore and London: Johns Hopkins University Press.

Bliss, M. (1983) *Brian De Palma*. New Jersey and London: Scarecrow Press.

Bloom, C. (ed.) (1998) *Gothic Horror*. Basingstoke and London: Macmillan.

Bronfen, E. (1998) *The Knotted Subject: Hysteria and its Discontents*. New Jersey: Princeton University Press.

Brownlow, K. (1990) *Behind the Mask of Innocence*. London: Jonathan Cape.

Burke, E. (1757) *A Philosophical Enquiry into our Ideas of the Sublime and Beautiful*. Oxford: Oxford University Press (revsd. edn. 1990).

Campbell, J. (1988) *The Hero With a Thousand Faces*. London and New York: Paladin.

Carroll, N. (1990) *The Philosophy of Horror*. London and New York: Routledge.

Cartmell, D., H. Kaye, I. Whelehan, I. Q. Hunter (eds) (1997) *Trash Aesthetics: Popular Culture and its Audience*. London: Pluto Press.

Chibnall, S. (1998) *Making Mischief: The Cult Films of Pete Walker*. London: FAB Press.

Clarens, C. (1967) *Horror Movies*. London: Secker and Warburg.

Cooke, A. (ed.) (1971) *Garbo and the Nightwatchman*. London: Secker and Warburg.

Dadoun, R. (1989) 'Fetishism in the Horror Film' in J. Donald (ed.) *Fantasy and the Cinema*. London: BFI, 39–63.

Darwin, C. (1859) *On the Origin of Species*. London: Watts & Co.

Dewe Mathews, T. (1994) *Censored: The Story of Film Censorship in Britain*. London: Chatto and Windus.

Diski, J. (1992) 'A Horrified Lidless Stare', *Sight and Sound*, Oct 1992, 2, 6, 35.

Doherty, T. (1988) *Teenagers and Teenpics: The Juvenilisation of American Movies in the 1950s*. London and Boston: Unwin Hyman.

Donald, J. (ed.) (1989) *Fantasy and the Cinema*. London: BFI.

Drew, W. (1984) *David Cronenberg*, BFI Dossier 21. London: BFI.

Durgnat, R. (1970) *A Mirror For England*. London: Faber and Faber.

Dyer, R. (1993) 'Dracula and Desire', *Sight and Sound*, Jan 1993, 3, 1, 8–15.

—— (1997) 'Kill and Kill Again', *Sight and Sound*, Sept 1997, 7, 9, 14–17.

Dyson, J. (1997) *Bright Darkness: The Lost Art of the Supernatural Horror Film*. London: Cassell.

Eaton, M. (1997) 'Born Again', *Sight and Sound*, Dec 1997, 7, 12, 6–9.

Eisner, L. (1973) *The Haunted Screen*. London: Secker and Warburg.

Elsaessar, T. (1989) 'Social Mobility and the Fantastic: German Silent Cinema' in J. Donald (ed.) *Fantasy and the Cinema*. London: BFI, 23–39.

Ferguson Ellis, K. (1989) *The Contested Castle*. Illinois: University of Illinois Press.

Frank, A. (1981) *Horror Films*. London: Optimum Books.

Frayling, C. (1991) *Vampyres: Lord Byron to Count Dracula*. London and Boston: Faber and Faber.

—— (1996) *The Birth of Horror*. London: BBC Books.

Freeland, C. (1995) 'Realist Horror' in C. Freeland and T. Wartenberg (eds) *Philosophy and Film*. London and New York, 126–35.

French, K. (ed.) (1996) *Screen Violence*. London: Bloomsbury.

Freud, S. (1985a) *Art and Literature* (revsd. edn.). London and New York: Pelican Books.

—— (1985b) *Civilisation, Society and Religion* (revsd. edn.). London and New York: Pelican Books.

—— (1985c) *The Interpretation of Dreams* (revsd. edn.). London and New York: Pelican Books.

Gelder, K. (1994) *Reading the Vampire*. London and New York: Routledge.

Grant, B. K. (ed.) (1984) *Planks of Reason: Essays on the Horror Film*. Metuchen, New Jersey: Scarecrow Press.

—— (ed.) (1996) *The Dread of Difference: Gender and the Horror Film*. Austin: University of Texas Press.

—— (1997) 'Rich and Strange: The Yuppie Horror Film' in S. Neale and M. Smith (eds) *Contemporary Hollywod Cinema*. London and New York: Routledge, 280–94.

Greene, G. (1980) *The Pleasure Dome*. Oxford and New York, OUP.

Grixti, J. (1989) *Terrors of Uncertainty*. London and New York: Routledge.

Halliwell, L. (1988) *The Dead That Walk*. London and New York: Paladin.

Handling, P. (ed.) (1983) *The Shape of Rage: The Films of David Cronenberg*. Toronto: General Publishing.

Hardy, P. (ed.) (1984) *The Encyclopaedia of Science Fiction Movies*. London: Aurum.

—— (ed.) (1985) *The Aurum Film Encyclopaedia: Horror*. London: Aurum.

Harryhausen, R. (1989) *The Film Fantasy Scrapbook*. London: Titan Books.

Hill, D. (1958) 'The Face of Horror', *Sight and Sound*, Winter 1958–1959, 6–11.

Hogan, D. (1986) *Dark Romance: Sex and Death in the Horror Film*. Jefferson and London: McFarland.

Holte, J. C. (1997) *Dracula in the Dark*. Westport and London: Greenwood Press.

Hunt, L. (1992) 'A Sadistic Night at the Opera', *Velvet Light Trap*, 30.

Jameson, F. (1992) *Signatures of the Visible*. London and New York: Routledge.

Jankovich, M. (1992) *Horror*. London: Batsford.

Jones, A. (1983) 'Argento', *Cinefantastique*, 13, 5, 20–22.

Jaworzyn, S. (1990) 'The Rat Will Improvise: Alejandro Jodorowsky', *Monthly Film Bulletin*, April 1990, 57, 675, 120.

Kermode, M. (1993) 'Ghoul School', *Sight and Sound*, June 1993, 3, 6, 10–12.

—— (1998) *The Exorcist*. London: BFI.

Kermode, M. and P. Kirkham (1994) 'Making *Frankenstein* and the Monster', *Sight and Sound*, Nov 1994, 4, 11, 6–9.

Kermode, M. and J. Petley (1998) 'The Censor and the State', *Sight and Sound*, May 1998, 8, 5, 14–16.

King, S. (1982) *Danse Macabre*. London and Sydney: Macdonald.

Kolocotroni, V., J. Goldman, O. Taxidou (eds) (1998) *Modernism*. Edinburgh: Edinburgh University Press.

Kracauer, S. (1947) *From Caligari to Hitler*. New Jersey: Princeton University Press.

Kristeva, J. (1982) *Powers of Horror: An Essay on Abjection*. New York: Columbia University Press.

Kuhn, A. (ed.) (1990) *Alien Zone*. London and New York: Verso.

Lake Crane, J. (1994) *Terror and Everyday Life: Singular Moments in the History of the Horror Film*. Thousand Oaks, London and New Delhi: Sage.

Leatherdale, C. (1985) *Dracula: The Novel and the Legend*. Wellingborough: Aquarian Press.

Lloyd, A. and D. Robinson (eds) (1983) *Movies of the Thirties*. London: Orbis.

Locanio, P. (1987) *Them or Us: Archetypal Interpretations of Fifties Alien Invasion Narratives*. Bloomington: Indiana University Press.

Marx, K. (1848) *The Communist Manifesto*.

McGilvray, D. (1988) 'Does Terror For Tots Make Sense?', *Film and Filming*, July 1988, 406, 24–7.

Mayersberg, P. (1980) 'The Overlook Hotel', *Sight and Sound*, Winter 1980/1981, 50, 1, 54–7.

Medved, M. (1994) *Hollywood vs America: Popular Culture and the War on Traditional Values*. New York: HarperCollins.

Milne, T. (1969) *Mamoullian*. London: Thames and Hudson.

Monaco, J. (1980) 'Aaaiieeeaarrggh!: horror movies', *Sight and Sound*, Spring 1980, 49, 2, 80–7.

Neale, S. (1980) *Genre*. London: BFI.

Newman, K. (ed.) (1997) *The BFI Companion to the Horror Film*. London: BFI/Cassell.

—— (1999a) *Catpeople*. London: BFI.

—— (1999b) *Millennium Movies*. London: Titan.

Nietzsche, F. (1838) *Twilight of the Gods/The Anti-Christ* (revsd. edn. 1986). London: Penguin.

O'Pray, M. (1989) 'Surrealism, Fantasy and the Grotesque: The Films of Jan Svankmajer' in
    J. Donald (ed.) *Fantasy and the Cinema*. London: BFI, 253–69.

Petrie, G. (1985) *Hollywood Destinies*. London and Boston: Routledge and Kegan Paul.

Phelps, G. (1975) *Film Censorship*. London: Gollancz

Pirie, D. (1973) *The Heritage of Horror: the English Gothic Cinema 1946–1972*. London: Gordon
    Fraser.

—— (1977) *The Vampire Cinema*. London: Gallery.

Prawer, S. S. (1980) *Caligari's Children*. Oxford and New York: OUP.

Prothero, D. (1997) 'Occult', *Sight and Sound*, Dec 1997, 7, 8, 24–26.

Rank, O. (1914) 'Der Doppelgänger', *Imago*, 3, viii–xii.

Radcliffe, A. (1826) 'On the Supernatural in Poetry', *New Monthly Magazine* 16.

Rebello, S. (1990) *Alfred Hitchcock and the Making of 'Psycho'*. New York: Dembner Books.

Ringel, H. (1975) 'Terence Fisher: The Human Side' in *Cinefantastique*, 4, 3, 5–18.

Ritzer, G. (1998) *The McDonaldisation Thesis*. London and Thousand Oaks: Sage.

Robb, B. J. (1998) *Screams and Nightmares*. London: Titan Books.

Robbins, H. (1993) 'More Human than I am Alone: Womb envy in David Cronenberg's *The Fly* and
    Dead Ringers' in S. Cohan and I. Rae Hark (eds) *Screening the Male*. London and New York:
    Routledge, 134–51.

Rodley, C. (ed.) (1992) *Cronenberg on Cronenberg*. London and Boston: Faber and Faber.

—— (1996) 'Crash', *Sight and Sound*, June 1996, 6, 6, 5–11.

Ronay, G. (1972) *The Vampire Myth*. London and Sydney: Pan Books.

Rosenbaum, J. (1980) 'The Rocky Horror Picture Cult', *Sight and Sound*, Spring 1980, 49, 2,
    78–80.

Rosenthal, S. (1975) *The Hollywood Professionals Vol. 4: Browning and Siegel*. London and New
    York: AS Barnes.

Rushing Hocker, J. (1995) 'Evolution of the "The New Frontier" in *Alien* and *Aliens*: Patriarchal Co-
    Optation of the Feminine Archetype', in J. Martin and Ostwalt, C. Jnr. (ed.) *Screening the
    Sacred*. Oxford and San Francisco: Westview Press, 94–119.

Russo, M. (1994) *The Female Grotesque*. London and New York: Routledge.

Salt, B. (1979) 'From Caligari to Who?', *Sight and Sound*, Spring 1979, 48, 2, 119–23.

Scapperotti, D. (1995) 'The Hunchback of Notre Dame' in *Cinefantastique*, 27, 10, 16–32.

Sconce, J. (1993) 'Spectacles of Death: Identification, Reflexivity, and Contemporary Horror' in J.
    Collins, H. Radner and A. Preacher-Collins (eds) *Film Theory Goes to the Movies*. London
    and New York: AFI/Routledge, 103–20.

Seltzer, M. (1998) *Serial Killers*. London and New York: Routledge.

Siegel, J. (1972) *Val Lewton: The Reality of Terror*. London: Secker and Warburg.

Skal, D. (1994) *The Monster Show: A Cultural History of Horror*. New York: W. W. Norton.

Sobchack, V. (1987) *Screening Space: The American Science Fiction Film*. New York: Ungar.

Staiger, J. (1993) 'Taboos and Totems: Cultural Meanings of *The Silence of the Lambs*' in J. Collins, H. Radner and A. Preacher-Collins (eds) *Film Theory Goes to the Movies*. London and New York: AFI/Routledge, 142–54.

Stanbrook, A. (1990) 'Invasion of the Purple People Eaters', *Sight and Sound*, Winter 1990/91, 60, 1, 48–50.

Taubin, A. (1991) 'Killing Men', *Sight and Sound*, May 1991, 1, 1, 14–19.

—— (1995) 'Bloody Tales', *Sight and Sound*, Jan 1995, 5, 1, 8–11.

Titterington, P. L. (1981) 'Kubrick and *The Shining*', *Sight and Sound*, Spring 1981, 50, 2, 117–21.

Traube, E. (1992) *Dreaming Identities*. Oxford and San Francisco: Westview Press.

Truffaut, F. (1986) *Hitchcock by Truffaut: The Definitive Study*. London: Paladin, 410–35.

Twitchell, J. (1985) *Dreadful Pleasures: An Anatomy of Modern Horror*. Oxford and New York: OUP.

Underwood, T. and C. Miller (eds) (1986) *Kingdom of Fear: The World of Stephen King*. London: New English Library/Hodder and Stoughton.

Vale, V. and A. Juno (eds) (1986) *Incredibly Strange Films*. London: Plexus.

Walker, B. (1978) 'Werner Herzog's *Nosferatu*', *Sight and Sound*, Autumn 1978, 47, 4, 202–5.

Warner, M. (1994) *From the Beast to the Blonde: On Fairytales and their Tellers*. London and Sydney: Chatto and Windus.

Weaver, T. (ed.) (1991) *Science Fiction Stars and Horror Heroes*. Jefferson and London: McFarland.

Wells, P. (1993) 'The Invisible Man: Shrinking Masculinity in the 1950s Sci-Fi 'B' Movie', in P. Kirkham and J. Thumin (eds) *Me Tarzan: Men, Masculinity and Movies*. London: Lawrence and Wishart, 181–99.

—— (1996) *Around the World In Animation*. London: BFI/MOMI.

—— (1998) *Understanding Animation*. London and New York: Routledge.

—— (1999a) 'Apocalypse Then!: The Ultimate Monstrosity and Strange Things on the Coast', in I. Q. Hunter (ed.) *Unearthly Strangers: The British Science Fiction Film*. London and New York: Routledge, 199–214.

—— (1999b) 'Thou Art Translated: Animated Adaptations' in D. Cartmell and I. Whelehan (eds) *Adaptations*. London and New York: Routledge, 48–57.

Wiater, S. (1992) *Dark Visions*. New York: Avon Books.

Wilson, C. and D. Seaman (1990) *The Serial Killers*. London: W. H. Allen.

Wilt, D. (1995) 'Horror from South of the Border', *Cinefantastique*, 27, 10, 40–8.

Williams, L. R. (1989) *Hardcore: Power, Pleasure and 'the Frenzy of the Visible'*. Berkeley: University of California.

Wood, R. (1986) *Hollywood: From Vietnam to Reagan*. New York: Columbia University Press.

—— (1989) *Hitchcock's Films Revisited*. London and Boston: Faber and Faber, 142–52.

Wood, R. and R. Lippe (eds) (1979) *American Nightmare: Essays on the Horror Film*. Toronto: Festival of Festivals.

Wright Wexman, V. (1985) *Roman Polanski*. London: Columbus Books.